ASPECTS OF THE NOVEL

EDWARD MORGAN FORSTER was born in London in 1879, attended Tonbridge School as a day boy, and went on to King's College, Cambridge, in 1897. With King's he had a lifelong connection and was elected to an Honorary Fellowship in 1946. He declared that his life as a whole had not been dramatic, and he was unfailingly modest about his achievements. Interviewed by the BBC on his eightieth birthday, he said: 'I have not written as much as I'd like to . . . I write for two reasons: partly to make money and partly to win the respect of people whom I respect . . . I had better add that I am quite sure that I am not a great novelist.' Eminent critics and the general public have judged otherwise and in his obituary *The Times* called him 'one of the most esteemed English novelists of his time'.

He wrote six novels, four of which appeared before the First World War, *Where Angels Fear to Tread* (1905), *The Longest Journey* (1907), *A Room With A View* (1908) and *Howards End* (1910). An interval of fourteen years elapsed before he published *A Passage to India*. It won both the Prix Femina Vie Heureuse and the James Tait Black Memorial Prize. *Maurice*, his novel on a homosexual theme, finished in 1914, was published posthumously in 1971. He also published two volumes of short stories; two collections of essays; a critical work, *Aspects of the Novel*; *The Hill of Devi*, a fascinating record of two visits Forster made to the Indian State of Dewas Senior; two biographies; two books about Alexandria (where he worked for the Red Cross in the First World War); and, with Eric Crozier, the libretto for Britten's opera *Billy Budd*. He died in June 1970.

OLIVER STALLYBRASS (1925–78) was educated at Winchester and Cambridge, and qualified in librarianship at the University of London. A distinguished editor, publisher and translator, he is best remembered for his Abinger Edition of the works of E. M. Forster.

FRANK KERMODE was born in 1919 and educated at Douglas High School and Liverpool University. From 1974 to 1982 he was King Edward VII Professor of English Literature at Cambridge University. He is an Honorary Fellow of King's College, Cambridge, and holds honorary doctorates from Chicago, Liverpool, Newcastle, Yale,

Wesleyan, Sewanee and Amsterdam universities. He is a Fellow of the British Academy and of the Royal Society of Literature, an Honorary Member of the American Academy of Arts and Sciences and of the American Academy of Arts and Letters, and an Officier de l'Ordre des Arts et des Sciences. He was knighted in 1991. Professor Kermode's publications include *Romantic Image*, *The Sense of an Ending*, *Puzzles and Epiphanies*, *Continuities*, *Shakespeare*, *Spenser*, *Donne*, *The Classic*, *The Genesis of Secrecy*, *Essays on Fiction 1971–82*, *Forms of Attention*, *History and Value*, *An Appetite for Poetry*, *The Uses of Error*, *Shakespeare's Language* and an autobiography, *Not Entitled*. He has also edited *He Knew He was Right* and *The Way We Live Now* by Anthony Trollope, and *The Figure in the Carpet and Other Stories* by Henry James for Penguin Classics.

E. M. FORSTER

Aspects of the Novel

Edited by OLIVER STALLYBRASS
with an Introduction by FRANK KERMODE

PENGUIN BOOKS

PENGUIN BOOKS

Published by the Penguin Group
Penguin Books Ltd, 80 Strand, London WC2R ORL, England
Penguin Group (USA) Inc., 375 Hudson Street, New York, New York 10014, USA
Penguin Group (Canada), 10 Alcorn Avenue, Toronto, Ontario, Canada M4V 3B2
(a division of Pearson Penguin Canada Inc.)
Penguin Ireland, 25 St Stephen's Green, Dublin 2, Ireland
(a division of Penguin Books Ltd)
Penguin Group (Australia), 250 Camberwell Road,
Camberwell, Victoria 3124, Australia (a division of Pearson Australia Group Pty Ltd)
Penguin Books India Pvt Ltd, 11 Community Centre, Panchsheel Park, New Delhi – 110 017, India
Penguin Group (NZ), cnr Airborne and Rosedale Roads, Albany,
Auckland 1310, New Zealand (a division of Pearson New Zealand Ltd)
Penguin Books (South Africa) (Pty) Ltd, 24 Sturdee Avenue, Rosebank 2196, South Africa

Penguin Books Ltd, Registered Offices: 80 Strand, London WC2R ORL, England

www.penguin.com

First published by Edward Arnold 1927
Published in Pelican Books 1962
Reset and reprinted from the Abinger Edition 1976
Reprinted in Penguin Books 1990
Reprinted in Penguin Classics 2000
Reprinted with a new Introduction, Further Reading and Chronology 2005

I

Copyright © The Provost and Scholars of King's College, Cambridge, 1927, 1974
Editor's Introduction and other editorial matter copyright © Oliver Stallybrass, 1974
Introduction and Further Reading copyright © Frank Kermode, 2005
Chronology copyright © David Leavitt, 2005
All rights reserved

Printed in England by Clays Ltd, St Ives plc
Set in Monotype Baskerville

E. M. Forster dedicated
Aspects of the Novel:

TO CHARLES MAURON

CONTENTS

CHRONOLOGY

1879 Edward Morgan Forster born in London on New Year's Day, the son of Edward Forster, an architect, and Marianne Thornton.

1897 Becomes a student of classics at King's College, Cambridge, having attended Tonbridge School (which he disliked).

1901 Death of Queen Victoria.

1903 Begins writing for the *Independent Review*, a left-wing magazine edited from Cambridge by his friends G. Lowes Dickinson and Nathaniel Wedd. Also became acquainted around this time with Leonard Woolf and was to remain on the fringes of the Bloomsbury Group. Because of an inheritance from his great-aunt, becomes financially independent.

1905 *Where Angels Fear to Tread.*

1907 Becomes a private tutor to Syed Ross Mahood, the dedicatee of *A Passage to India*, with whom he probably falls in love.
The Longest Journey.

1908 *A Room with a View.*

1910 *Howards End.*

1911 *The Celestial Omnibus.*

1912 Visits India.

1913–14 Writes *Maurice* (published posthumously in 1971, at his request) and starts work on *A Passage to India*.

1914–18 First World War.
As a pacifist refuses to fight and instead moves to Alexandria, Egypt, where he works as a medical orderly.

1919 Opposition to the British rule suppressed in the

Punjab (Amritsar Massacre). Indian-run ministerial administrations introduced in selected fields.

Returns to England and works as literary editor for the left-wing newspaper the *Daily Herald*.

1921 Revisits India, and writes a travel memoir, *The Hill of Devi*; resumes the writing of *A Passage to India*.

1922 James Joyce, *Ulysses*; T. S. Eliot, *The Waste Land*; Virginia Woolf, *Jacob's Room*.

1924 *A Passage to India*, published to great acclaim.

1927 Gives a series of lectures in Cambridge, published as *Aspects of the Novel*.

1928 *The Eternal Moment*, a second collection of stories, is Forster's last published work of fiction in his lifetime. For the next forty years he works as a critic and broadcaster.

1929 Great Depression begins with the collapse of the New York Stock Exchange.

1934 *Goldsworthy Lowes Dickinson*, a biography.

1936 *Abinger Harvest*, a collection of essays.

1939–45 Second World War.

1946 Elected to an Honorary Fellowship at King's College, Cambridge.

1947 Indian Independence Act. Pakistan and East Pakistan (now Bangladesh) created as Muslim states.

1948 Assassination of Mahatma Gandhi.

1951 Helps to write the libretto for Benjamin Britten's opera *Billy Budd*, based on a sea story by Herman Melville.

Two Cheers for Democracy, a collection of essays.

1953 Abinger Edition of collected works.

1956 *Marianne Thornton*, a biography.

1960 Appears as a witness for the defence in the trial for D. H. Lawrence's suppressed novel, *Lady Chatterley's Lover*; it is cleared of obscenity charges and published.

1967 Relaxation of laws on homosexual behaviour in England and Wales.

1970 Dies 7 June, aged 91.
1971 *Maurice.*
1972 *The Life to Come.*

INTRODUCTION

As Oliver Stallybrass makes clear in his editorial introduction, E. M. Forster was pleased but a little apprehensive at the prospect of giving the Clark Lectures. At forty-eight he had earned a high reputation as a novelist, and it was primarily as a novelist that he thought of himself: to write good novels was 'the chief point of [his] being alive.'[1] His first novel, *Where Angels Fear to Tread*, was published in 1905, when he was twenty-six. It was followed by *The Longest Journey* (1907), *A Room With a View* (1908) and *Howards End* (1910). In 1913 he wrote his homosexual novel *Maurice*, which remained unpublished and known only within an intimate circle until 1971. Finally, after a long gap, he finished and published his most successful work, *A Passage to India* (1924). A year or two later, as he read in preparation for the Clark Lectures, he must have been conscious of his place among the most respected novelists of the day. But he was also aware that he was no longer writing novels, and feared that he might never do so again. He was now required to lecture *about* novels, to become a critic – a profession for which he had limited respect. However, he was a critic who knew how to write novels, and his practitioner's knowledge of the craft was what would distinguish him from his Cambridge audience.

The occasion was nevertheless a daunting one. His benefactors, the Trinity fellowship, were a formidable body of men, including the philosopher G. E. Moore, whom Forster knew well, and the great scholar poet, A. E.

1. Stallybrass's Introduction, p. xxii.

Housman, whom he greatly admired. During his discussion of time and value (p. 42) he quotes two lines from Housman's fine gloomy poem 'Eight O'Clock' – 'And then the clock collected in the tower / Its strength, and struck' – without quotation marks, and not set as verse – perhaps intending a veiled tribute to the poet in the audience.[2]

Forster chose to use an informal, 'indeed talkative' tone, but his whimsy, so irritating to some severer critics, is often used to mask a sense of the speaker's difference – in temperament and qualification – from his audience. Some of them, perhaps most or all of them, are pseudo-scholars and not true readers, readers who 'sit down and struggle with the writer'. Pseudo-scholars, a class that includes professors who have written large books on the novel as well as all the people who read superficially, do not even begin the struggle.

This mild, masked contempt arises from a conviction that novels, like other works of art, may be consumed and even praised by non-novelists who haven't the slightest conception of their art. A character in *The Longest Journey* complains that her future husband is wilfully obscure. 'Couldn't you make your stories more obvious? Uncle Willy floundered helplessly' (ch. 15). Reviewing the book, the critic Edward Garnett sympathized: 'it is not easy to explain the subtle quality of Mr Forster's brilliant novel to Uncle Willy and his kinsfolk . . . How can the art of telling, this network woven of a succession of tiny touches, be brought home to Uncle Willy?' Thanking Garnett for the review, Foster complained that 'the Uncle Willies are encompassing me sorely'.

The difficulty, shared by many artist-novelists in the early years of the twentieth century – Henry James, Joseph

2. 'Eight O'Clock' was published in *Last Poems* (1922). Housman attended at least two of the lectures – see p. 175. Other unattributed quotations are from Wordsworth (p. 95) and Meredith (p. 105).

Conrad, Ford Madox Ford – was to reconcile their art, the art of telling, with the financially desirable feat of giving Uncle Willy a good plain read. Forster's devotion to that succession of tiny touches – what in *Aspects* he calls 'rhythm' – frustrated Uncle Willy yet was rarely noticed by anybody else. *A Passage to India* won much acclaim, but not for its exquisite use of 'rhythm'. It was praised or blamed for its representation of relations between the Indians and their British occupiers, for the deftness or implausibility of the plot. Only a few reviewers felt that something else was going on, something more akin to poetry than politics. Forster set a high value on novels in which something else was going on, always unobserved by Uncle Willy but by supposedly better qualified readers, too.

Aspects of the Novel is the work of a practised artist address-ing a presumably rather superior selection of Uncle Willy and their betters; or, as F. R. Leavis expressed it, 'sillier dons' wives'[3] and, possibly, Kingsmen. Under the drollery, the little epigrams, the modesty, there is a strong claim to authority. We may say that the famous distinction between flat and round characters is too simple, and that the rela-tion of story to plot is glib or obvious; but in considering matters such as these Forster is saying something important in a way that the non-artists may find acceptable. He thinks it essential to understand the ways in which fiction can somehow give us the interior life of characters, reflected in what he calls the 'rotundity' of their presentation. He also thinks it important that in turning into plot the story acquires a complexity favourable to the creation of what he calls 'value'.

This term seems vague and unsatisfactory, referring as it does to 'something which is measured not by minutes or hours, but by intensity'. We know from our own experience

3. Quoted in Stallybrass's Introduction, p. xxiii.

what it is to be visited by moments quite out of the ordinary, quite other than those under the control of time. Forster says the story narrates 'the life in time', but the novel as a whole, 'if it is a good novel', includes the life by 'values' as well. This life consists not only of certain moments of ecstasy or vision but also of a sort of plenitude – perhaps even of its opposite, its negative – what Rebecca West in her review of *A Passage to India* was trying to specify when she spoke of a 'sacramental quality'.[4] Now this quality cannot be got in plain narrative. It can only arise from the whole complex structure, and is partly dependent on 'rhythm'.

One wonders whether, in depending on the expression 'value', Forster may have been thinking, perhaps vaguely, for he did not aspire to philosophy, of the philosophy or talk of G. E. Moore. The novel has to be an aesthetic object, has to possess beauty; and Forster can say how such objects come into being, and how 'rhythm' enables them to have their proper effect. It cannot be imposed from the outside and is not available to writers who plan their books beforehand. It must grow. It may depend on effects as evanescent as those of Proust's *phrase de Vinteuil*, celebrated by Forster in some of the best passages of these lectures (p. 48). And in the end the effect of 'rhythm' can only be understood as analogous to the effects of music.

The single most impressive moment in the lectures, I think, is the discussion of the passage from *The Brothers Karamazov*. Forster quotes it at length, ostensibly to contrast its strange spirituality with the slightly embarrassing Christian fervour of the extract from *Adam Bede* which precedes it. (He could have done better by George Eliot and chosen the great passage in *Middlemarch* when Dorothea

4. Review printed in *E. M. Forster: The Critical Heritage*, ed. Philip Gardner, 1973, pp. 253–6; the words quoted are on p. 236.

returns from her wedding journey to Rome, but he will not admit even *Middlemarch* to the company of the greatest 'prophetic' novels.) What he seizes on in the account of Mitya's awakening is its beautiful unpredictability: some-one had provided him with a pillow, and 'his whole soul is quivering with tears . . . 'I've had a good dream, gentlemen,' he said in a strange voice, with a new light, as of joy, in his face' (pp. 118ff). This strange intensity is an example of the phenomenon for which Forster chose the approximation 'value' (p. 42). What matters most is that the lecturer should struggle to explain why, with these words, 'the tremendous current suddenly flows'. This is more to it than the be-littling of George Eliot and Dinah's Christianity. Here, if anywhere, one finds an argument in defence of Forster's conviction that even the greatest of English novels will be seen as 'little mansions . . . if we stand them for an instant in the colonnades of *War and Peace*, or the vaults of *The Brothers Karamazov*' (p. 27).

The harshness of Dr Leavis's judgement (pp. xxiii–xxiv) may be seen as in part a consequence of Cambridge aca-demic feuding, in part as a teacher's irritation at the circu-lation of neat formulas that become, in the hands of students, substitutes for critical thinking. But that harshness is also the revenge of the critic on the artist. Forster invites such reprisals with his coy defensiveness, his not very secret conviction that the study of the novel as a form of art requires the mind and hand of a practitioner, and his belief that the task of discussing such matters as 'rhythm' before an audience of non-serious readers calls for the deployment of all manner of witticisms and simplifications.

Aspects was a gratifying success as a lecture series, and it soon took its place among the best books about the novel. A great many books on that subject, more serious, more com-prehensive, more modern, have succeeded it, but it has not been replaced, simply because it is the work of an artist, and, for all its sometimes tiresome drolleries, it continues to demand the same measure of attention that we accord the Prefaces of Henry James.

FRANK KERMODE

FURTHER READING

OTHER WORKS BY FORSTER
Collected Short Stories (London: Penguin Books, 2002).
Howards End (Harmondsworth: Penguin Books, 2000).
The Longest Journey (Harmondsworth: Penguin Books, 2001).
Maurice (Harmondsworth: Penguin Books, 2000).
A Passage to India (Harmondsworth: Penguin Books, 2000).
'The *raison d'être* of criticism in the arts', in *Two Cheers for Democracy* (Harmondsworth: Penguin Books, 1965).
A Room with a View (Harmondsworth: Penguin Books, 2000).
Where Angels Fear to Tread (Harmondsworth: Penguin Books, 2001).

BIOGRAPHY
P. N. Furbank, *E. M. Forster: A Life*, 2 vols. (London: Secker & Warburg, 1977–8).

LETTERS
Selected Letters, ed. Mary Lago and P. N. Furbank, 2 vols. (Cambridge: Harvard University Press, 1983–5).

RECEPTION HISTORY
E. M. Forster: The Critical Heritage, ed. Philip Gardner (London: Routledge and Kegan Paul, 1973).

CRITICISM
E. K. Brown, *Rhythm in the Novel* (Toronto: University of Toronto Press, 1950).
Wilfred Stone, *The Cave and the Mountain: A Study of E. M. Forster* (Stanford: Stanford University Press), 1966.

EDITOR'S INTRODUCTION

It was Forster's annual custom, as one year passed into the next, to review in his diary the year just ended, presenting for his own inspection a balance-sheet of his physical and spiritual health, fame, and occasionally fortune. His pen ran more readily, on these occasions, to self-castigation and self-pity than to their opposites; and 1927 was accordingly a

difficult year to review as I feel happy and think it has been ... Substructure of money and fame. Gave away about £600 and could have managed more. Lectures (Jan.-March, published Oct.) a success. Big audiences in the Arts Theatre[1] and fellowship at King's in consequence.

The lectures were the annual Clark Lectures, sponsored by Trinity College, Cambridge, and of all such series in the field of English literature perhaps the best-known. From Leslie Stephen and Edmund Gosse to William Empson and I. A. Richards, the lecturers have included not only the predictable roll-call of famous, or once famous, critics and scholars, but also, over the last fifty or sixty years, the occasional noted practitioner of one of the literary arts – a historian, say, or a dramatist, or a poet. In the academic year 1926–7 the honour fell, for the first time, to a novelist; and the man selected was the author of that much-praised recent novel, *A Passage to India*.

Forster was pleased by the invitation, but hesitant over accepting; and on 17 March 1926 he wrote to his Indian friend Syed Ross Masood:

1. [Not today's (Cambridge) Arts Theatre, but a university lecture-hall then known by that name.]

I am in some excitement over the Clark Lectureship which has just been offered me by Trinity College, Cambridge – 8 lectures on English literature to be delivered there this autumn or next spring for the very substantial remuneration of £200. I shall accept if I can summon up courage.[2]

On the one hand there was the money, the uneasy knowledge that he was not writing another novel or anything else of substance, and above all, perhaps, the kudos – not least that of following in the footsteps of T. S. Eliot, for whose poetry Forster felt a strong if guarded admiration. (For that of A. E. Housman his feeling was unqualified; but it was probably a little later before he learned of Housman's having been offered the lectureship ahead of Eliot, and was allowed not merely to see but to copy Housman's elegant letter of refusal.)[3] On the other hand there were the factors calling for 'courage': chief among them, surely, not the ordeal of addressing a large and primarily academic audience, but the fear that in doing so, and on the subject of that 'inoffensive hen' the novel – for however the invitation was framed he must have known what was expected of him – he would be inviting, not least from his fellow novelists, the charge of inconsistency. For much of his life Forster was conscious of 'the gulf between the critical and creative states';[4] and when, twenty years after delivering the Clark Lectures, he was invited to that other Cambridge to speak on 'The *Raison d'Être* of Criticism', he began with the unreluctant admission that 'the case *against* criticism is alarm-

2. From a typewritten copy in the possession of Mr P. N. Furbank.

3. The letter – in which Housman courteously declines to let 'a whole year (and it would not take less)' be 'subtracted from those minute and pedantic studies in which I am fitted to excel, and which give me pleasure' – appears in full in Forster's Commonplace Book (following the block of entries which form Appendix A in the present volume) and in *The Letters of A. E. Housman*, edited by Henry Maas (London, Hart-Davis, 1971).

4. *Two Cheers for Democracy* (Abinger Edition, vol. 11), p. 118.

ingly strong' and concluded with the assertion that there *is* no 'first-class *raison d'être* for criticism in the arts'.[5] Such critical work as, holding these views, he nevertheless produced is, with no other exceptions, diminutive in scale, wayward in manner, and characterized by quick, sharp insights rather than by detailed analysis, or the consistent application of any critical theory, or the kind of dissection that might be looked for in a course of eight lectures 'on some period or periods of English Literature not earlier than Chaucer'.[6] Did he really wish to compete with Mr Clayton Hamilton, of whose *Materials and Methods of Fiction* he had made savage fun a few years back,[7] or with Professor E. A. Baker, a volume of whose monumental *History of the English Novel* he was presently to treat with a degree of disrespect that moved the author to an indignant protest, and Forster to a partial apology?[8]

The answer was, perhaps, never seriously in doubt: his current affluence might prove a mere flash in the American pan (the American sales of *A Passage to India* had far outstripped the British), unlike Housman he had no 'studies', pedantic or otherwise, to interrupt, and in the last resort he would have needed, for a refusal, a good deal less vanity, or vanity of an austerer or more sophisticated brand. Nevertheless, his acceptance did not entirely dispel his qualms,

5. *Op. cit.*, pp. 105, 118.

6. Forster's wording (quoted from p. 24) is not quite that of the terms of the lectureship as announced in the *Cambridge University Reporter*, 6 March 1883. But the terms have in fact varied from time to time: originally the lecturer was appointed for three years, had to give at least *sixty* lectures in all, and received £300 per annum. Forster had, of course, lectured on literary subjects before now; but his early series of Extension Lectures had been on Italian history, while his papers to the Working Men's College are rather a special case.

7. In the review which forms Appendix B and is the source of the phrase 'inoffensive hen'.

8. *The Spectator*, 28 June 1930, p. 1055, and 12 July 1930, p. 54.

some of which he voiced in a letter of 11 July to a friend in Alexandria, G. H. Ludolf:

I suppose the chief point in my being alive – at least the only public point – is to produce good books, which I can't say I'm doing. I spend my time in reading novels by other people in connection with some lectures to be given at Cambridge next year ... I ... am struggling through *Clarissa Harlowe*. Have just polished off Defoe and Sterne, both of whom I enjoy enormously. All this is pleasant enough, and the lectures are well paid. But it hasn't anything to do with creation. I feel like a dummy, from whom real life has been withdrawn, and I always have thought – and fear I always shall think – that most men over forty are in the same case: they are happy and pleasant enough, they enjoy things, they fill a place (having first made it to fill): but the respect they conspire to retain is totally misplaced.

The 'polishing off' of eighteenth-century novels had begun, probably in April, with *Tristram Shandy* and *Moll Flanders*, entries on which open the series of notes in Forster's Commonplace Book. Having got so far, on 17 May he wrote to Virginia Woolf, confessing that *Tristram* and *Moll* were new to him, and asking innocently for 'the names of the best novels'.[9] Even if he hadn't read all of them, I suspect that he had a clearer idea of what they might be than he chose to let on. In any case, since presently he was dismissing one of Virginia Woolf's published opinions as a 'dreary Bloomsbury conclusion',[10] it seems unlikely that he was unduly influenced by her private recommendations, if indeed she made any in response to this appeal.

If in advance Forster was 'fussed' by the 'somewhat agitating honour' of his lectures, the first 'went better than I expected', after the second he felt the audience was 'interested so far', by the third the lectures were 'a popular success among the Cambridge intelliganzanettes', by the

9. I have seen only a transcription of this letter.
10. See p. 164.

seventh a 'great success', and by the end 'the *greatest* success', so that 'my constant rise to fame impedes me' from letter-writing.[11] That the lectures were greatly enjoyed by most of the audience seems beyond a doubt – though this is explained in very different terms by the two correspondents who have been good enough to send me their recollections.[12] Mr George Rylands, who attended several of the lectures, recalls Forster's 'sly smile which quickly broke into a choking almost childish laugh' and adds:

Morgan never pontificated; he was never doctrinaire; never condescending or supercilious. Above all, although he never raised his voice, he never mumbled. The lectures, as he says in the printed version, were 'informal, indeed talkative' . . . The best of the Clark lecturers who followed him have succeeded for the same reason. They have talked, as Morgan was to do most memorably on the air . . . they talked to 'the Common Reader'.

This, the evidence of a Fellow of King's, would presumably be ruled out of court by my other correspondent, Dr F. R. Leavis, who sat through all eight lectures and remembers being 'astonished at the intellectual nullity that characterized them'. For him, the explanation of Forster's 'demonstratively sympathetic reception' and 'gruesome' success with his – 'certainly *his*' – capacity audience is that the latter consisted largely of 'sillier dons' wives and their friends' (Forster's 'intelliganzanettes'?), although there were also 'a great number of male dons present, including my old tutor (a Kingsman) – no exception to the rule that Kingsmen are always loyal'. Dr Leavis, who sees all this as

11. Letters to Virginia Woolf, 19 November 1926; C. P. Cavafy, 19 January 1927; Dora Carrington, 25 January 1927; Edward Arnold, 2 February 1927; T. E. Lawrence, 7 February 1927; E. V. Thompson, 10 March 1927; and T. E. Lawrence, 18 March 1927. For some of these quotations I am indebted, once again, to notes made by Mr P. N. Furbank.

12. Professor (then Mr) I. A. Richards proved to have been away from Cambridge at the time on a 'round-the-world honeymoon wander'.

evidencing 'the potent orthodoxy of enlightenment', continues:

The resultant book at once became a nuisance: all the girls' school English mistresses in England seized on the distinction between flat and round characters – which after all was as good as anything the book did yield critically. I speak as one who was largely responsible for the 'English' teaching at Girton and Newnham.

One may remark in passing that Dr Leavis has elsewhere found *Aspects of the Novel*[13] less wholly devoid of critical yield, Forster's 'necessary demolition-work' on Meredith having saved the author of *The Great Tradition*[14] from this particular necessity. But Dr Leavis is not the only critic who has been severe on *Aspects*, and it is time to consider the shortcomings with which it has been taxed.

Forster, as I have already suggested, was to some extent in a false position: that of a hired critic who had grave doubts about the value of criticism. From this dilemma he sought to extricate himself by offering criticism of the kind he found most congenial and 'inoffensive', casting occasional doubts over 'the whole caboodle', and firing off an early broadside against the 'pseudo-scholarship' of which he ironically claimed to be a practitioner. Was his position equivocal? J. D. Beresford thought it was: Forster, he says in his review of the book,[15] gives the impression that

for two pins he would have thrown his cap and gown over the windmill and declared that there wasn't a single principle among all the canons of literary criticism that was worth two-pence ... But anarchy cannot be openly preached in a University hall, not even literary anarchy, and Mr Forster had to respect the wishes

13. The title under which the lectures were published, in London by Edward Arnold and in New York by Harcourt, Brace, on 20 October 1927.
14. London, Chatto & Windus, 1948; see p. 33 in the Penguin edition.
15. *New Adelphi*, June 1928, pp. 366–7.

of the late William George Clark. Discretion was essential, a measure of sedateness . . .

If for Beresford, as I infer, the regrettable feature was the sedateness, for Ford Madox Ford it was the anarchism, and the irreverence that went with it. The title of his review, 'Cambridge on the Caboodle',[16] expresses his outrage at Forster's jesting use of that word. He equates Forster's attitude towards 'the art and craft that has given him honour and fame' with that of *Punch* 'towards the graver problems of life', and continues:

In as much as Mr Forster is a novelist he is a priest and in this work it is as if with the one hand he elevates the Host whilst with the other he writes donnish witticisms about how the sacred wafers are baked.

Forster the intellectual nullity, Forster the pusillanimous anarchist, Forster the sacrilegious priest: such are the charges that fly around when the novelist turns from creation to criticism – and takes with him the characteristic 're-fusal to be great' which is generally[17] regarded as amiable or even admirable in his fiction. But surely it is a mistake to measure Forster's slim volume by the standard of books he did not aspire to write or emulate? And it may be that a more pertinent criticism is the one made by the narrator in Somerset Maugham's *Cakes and Ale*:

I read *The Craft of Fiction* by Mr Percy Lubbock, from which I learned that the only way to write novels was like Henry James; after that I read *Aspects of the Novel* by Mr E. M. Forster, from which I learned that the only way to write novels was like Mr E. M. Forster . . .

For me, that disposes definitively of Lubbock's book; and, if I find it less than fair to Forster's, at least it suggests, in its

16. *Saturday Review of Literature*, 17 December 1927, pp. 449–50.
17. Though not by Lionel Trilling, who coined the phrase (*E. M. Forster*, London, Hogarth Press, 1944, pp. 10, 155).

amusingly exaggerated way, what kind of a book *Aspects of the Novel* is: a set of observations, somewhat arbitrarily arranged (the first hint of the framework for Forster's 'ramshackly course' occurs only towards the end of the notes which form Appendix A), of a man who is a novelist first, a slightly uncommon reader second, a friend third, and an analytical or theorizing critic fourth. Friend third and critic fourth. For it has to be admitted that Forster never hesitated to subordinate criticism to friendship, and in *Aspects of the Novel* there are three clear examples: the gratuitous puff (neither his first nor his last) for Dickinson's *The Magic Flute*; the discrepancy between his lukewarm private and fulsome published comments[18] on two of Percy Lubbock's books, a discrepancy almost certainly reflecting loyalty and gratitude to a King's contemporary who in 1918, as his superior in the Red Cross, had given him strong support in an organizational dispute; and his decision 'not to send Mrs Woolf the uncorrected proofs for a small private reason; they contain a criticism of her own work which I have modified in the revise!!'[19] We have the right to be scandalized – Forster's word in the context of his famous preference for betraying his country rather than his friend – but not to be surprised: People before Art was a lifelong and oft-stated part of his credo.

Even when seen for what it is, *Aspects of the Novel* still has the occasional power to madden – as Forster intended it should: 'I hope that I have annoyed some of you over Scott!' he remarks. Scott's admirers have duly risen to the bait,[20] voices have been raised in favour of many another

18. See pp. 81, 136, 137, 160–61. And as late as 1944 Forster was recommending *The Craft of Fiction* to his Indian listeners; see the disappointingly repetitive talk, 'The Art of Fiction', which forms Appendix D.

19. Letter to Brian Fagan (Forster's editor at Edward Arnold), 2 September 1927.

20. Notably several of the book's reviewers: in order of their general friendliness, L. P. Hartley (*Saturday Review*, 17 December 1927), Virginia

target, and Jamesians have defended the Master at anything up to eight times the length of Forster's attack.[21] It is
a dreary work of criticism that provokes no grumbles; here
are a few of my own. Starting with James, does not *he*, if anyone, have a real and powerful sense of evil (see p. 128), even
if (possibly) he never actually uses the word? Is it fair to let
George Eliot be represented by *Adam Bede*, Conrad by
Marlow, Mrs Gaskell by a mere mention of *Cranford*?
(Partial answer: Forster quotes from *Adam Bede* for other
ends than 'fairness'. Still, he can also be genuinely unfair,
as when he presents *Materials and Methods of Fiction* as an
even sillier book than it is.)[22] And, if this is not an unfair
question, why have I wasted precious time reading *Flecker's
Magic*, a feeble piece of whimsy that lacks even the neat
coherence of Forster's admiring summary, and is not even
(it seems) by one of his friends?

Strong disagreement with a lively, provocative critic is, of
course, both more pleasurable and more profitable than
tepid agreement with a dull one: even the notorious distinction between flat and round characters, shaky as it is and
backed by shakier examples, has by reason of those very
facts led to some useful fresh thinking on the subject, notably
by Edwin Muir.[23] But it would be quite wrong to suggest
that the pleasures offered by *Aspects* are principally those of
dissent. What most readers will cherish are the numerous
particular judgements, instinctive rather than intellectual,

Woolf (*Nation and Athenaeum*, 12 November 1927), and E. F. Benson
(*Spectator*, 29 October 1927). All three reviews may be found in that
valuable compilation, *E. M. Forster: The Critical Heritage*, edited by
Philip Gardner (London, Routledge & Kegan Paul, 1973).

21. See, for example, Geoffrey Tillotson, *Criticism and the Nineteenth
Century* (London, Athlone Press, 1951, pp. 244–69).

22. Compare Forster's treatment of it (pp. 29–30, 176–8) with the
extracts from it which form Appendix C.

23. *The Structure of the Novel* (London, Hogarth Press, 1928).

that hit their nail lightly but very precisely and often wittily on the head; the striking juxtapositions, particularly those of Sterne and Virginia Woolf, *Adam Bede* and *The Brothers Karamazov* (that of Richardson and Henry James strikes me as plain perverse);[24] the series of challenges to think hard about some not fully developed idea; and, though Forster never once mentions his own novels, the frequent illuminations of his fictional aims and achievements.[25] All this makes *Aspects of the Novel*, still, an excellent introduction to its subject, and a useful adjunct to other, more sustained and consistent works of criticism.

The text of this volume is that of the Abinger Edition published by Edward Arnold in 1974, which was based on a word-by-word collation of earlier editions and of various manuscript fragments at King's College, Cambridge. The most significant feature revealed by this collation was the existence of numerous small differences between the first (and subsequent) British and American editions. During March 1927 Forster sent typescripts both to Arnold in London and to Harcourt, Brace in New York; and it is clear that he made corrections to the Arnold typescript or proofs or both which were not transmitted across the Atlantic, or were transmitted too late. It is equally clear, however, that the Arnold edition of 1927 (and hence subse-

24. Wilfred Stone has suggested (*The Cave and the Mountain: A Study of E. M. Forster*, Stanford and London, Stanford University Press and Oxford University Press, 1966, p. 119) that Forster's prolonged quarrel with James may have stemmed from an unfortunate early encounter. Can it be that the far-fetched comparison between James and Richardson was made for the sole purpose of enabling Forster to parody James's style and tax him with snobbery?

25. Most strikingly in the case of 'rhythm', a concept fruitfully applied to Forster's own novels by, notably, E. K. Brown (*Rhythm in the Novel*, University of Toronto Press, 1950) and James McConkey (*The Novels of E. M. Forster*, Ithaca, Cornell University Press, 1957).

quent British editions) is not without blemish; and at some two dozen points it has been emended, some of the emendations being suggested or confirmed by the American edition, or (in one apparent instance of revision by Forster) by later British and American editions, or by the manuscript. In addition, Forster's quotations from other authors have been checked and, where necessary, corrected; and the principle of accurate quotation has been extended to include accurate citation of authors, titles and dates of publication. Footnotes are normally Forster's; editorial interpolations are recognizable as such by being enclosed in square brackets. Full details of these and other textual matters are given in the Abinger Edition.

In the Abinger Edition I expressed, and I would like here to repeat, albeit in more summary form, my thanks for help received from many people at King's College, Cambridge (particularly those named below), and from the following individuals: Mrs Patricia Bradford, Mrs Penelope Bulloch, Miss Laurie Cherbonnier, Mr P. N. Furbank, Dr F. R. Leavis, Mr Donald Loukes, Mr T. S. Matthews, Mr Simon Nowell-Smith, Professor I. A. Richards, Mr George Rylands, Mrs Beth Schneiderman, and my wife, Mrs Gunnvor Stallybrass.

OLIVER STALLYBRASS

AUTHOR'S NOTE

THESE are some lectures (the Clark Lectures) which were delivered under the auspices of Trinity College, Cambridge, in the spring of 1927. They were informal, indeed talkative, in their tone, and it seemed safer when presenting them in book form not to mitigate the talk, in case nothing should be left at all. Words such as 'I', 'you', 'one', 'we', 'curiously enough', 'so to speak', 'only imagine' and 'of course' will consequently occur on every page and will rightly distress the sensitive reader; but he is asked to remember that if these words were removed others, perhaps more distinguished, might escape through the orifices they left, and that since the novel is itself often colloquial it may possibly withhold some of its secrets from the graver and grander streams of criticism, and may reveal them to backwaters and shallows.

I

INTRODUCTORY

THIS lectureship is connected with the name of William George Clark, a Fellow of Trinity. It is through him we meet today, and through him we shall approach our subject.

Clark was, I believe, a Yorkshireman. He was born in 1821, was at school at Sedbergh and Shrewsbury, entered Trinity as an undergraduate in 1840, became Fellow four years later, and made the college his home for nearly thirty years, only leaving it when his health broke, shortly before his death. He is best known as a Shakespearean scholar, but he published two books on other subjects to which we must here refer. He went as a young man to Spain and wrote a pleasant lively account of his holiday called *Gazpacho*: gazpacho being the name of a certain cold soup which he ate and appears to have enjoyed among the peasants of Andalusia; indeed he appears to have enjoyed everything. Eight years later, as a result of a holiday in Greece, he published a second book, *Peloponnesus*. *Peloponnesus* is a graver work and a duller. Greece was a serious place in those days, more serious than Spain, besides, Clark had by now not only taken Orders but become Public Orator, and he was, above all, travelling with Dr Thompson, the then Master of the college, who was not at all the sort of person to be involved in a cold soup. The jests about mules and fleas are consequently few, and we are increasingly confronted with the remains of classical antiquity and the sites of battles. What survives in the book – apart from its learning – is its feeling for Greek countryside. Clark also travelled in Italy and Poland.

To turn to his academic career. He planned the great Cambridge Shakespeare, first with Glover, then with Aldis Wright (both librarians of Trinity), and, helped by Aldis Wright, he issued the popular Globe Shakespeare. He collected much material for an edition of Aristophanes. He also published some sermons, but in 1869 he gave up Holy Orders – which, by the way, will exempt us from excessive orthodoxy. Like his friend and biographer Leslie Stephen, like Henry Sidgwick and others of that generation, he did not find it possible to remain in the Church, and he has explained his reasons in a pamphlet entitled *The Present Dangers of the Church of England.* He resigned his post of Public Orator in consequence, while retaining his college tutorship. He died at the age of fifty-seven, esteemed by all who knew him as a lovable, scholarly and honest man. You will have realized that he is a Cambridge figure. Not a figure in the great world or even at Oxford, but a spirit peculiar to these courts, which perhaps only you who tread them after him can justly appreciate: the spirit of integrity. Out of a bequest in his will, his old college has provided for a series of lectures, to be delivered annually 'on some period or periods of English Literature not earlier than Chaucer', and to be connected with his name.

Invocations are out of fashion, yet I wanted to make this small one, for two reasons. Firstly, may a little of Clark's integrity be with us through this course; and secondly, may he accord us a little inattention! For I am not keeping quite strictly to the terms laid down. 'Period or periods of English Literature.' This condition, though it sounds liberal and is liberal enough in spirit, happens verbally not quite to suit our subject, and the introductory lecture will be occupied in explaining why this is. The points raised may possibly seem trivial. But they will lead us to a convenient vantage-post from which we can begin our main attack.

We need a vantage-post, for the novel is a formidable mass, and it is so amorphous – no mountain in it to climb, no Parnassus or Helicon, not even a Pisgah. It is most distinctly one of the moister areas of literature – irrigated by a hundred rills and occasionally degenerating into a swamp. I do not wonder that the poets despise it, though they sometimes find themselves in it by accident. And I am not surprised at the annoyance of the historians when by accident it finds itself among them. Perhaps we ought to define what a novel is before starting. This will not take a second. M. Abel Chevalley has, in his brilliant little manual,[1] provided a definition, and if a French critic cannot define the English novel who can? It is, he says, 'a fiction in prose of a certain extent' (*une fiction en prose d'une certaine étendue*). That is quite good enough for us, and we may perhaps go so far as to add that the extent should not be less than 50,000 words. Any fictitious prose work over 50,000 words will be a novel for the purposes of these lectures, and if this seems to you unphilosophic will you think of an alternative definition, which will include *The Pilgrim's Progress, Marius the Epicurean, The Adventures of a Younger Son, The Magic Flute, A Journal of the Plague Year, Zuleika Dobson, Rasselas, Ulysses* and *Green Mansions*, or else will give reasons for their exclusion? Parts of our spongy tract seem more fictitious than other parts, it is true: near the middle, on a tump of grass, stand Miss Austen with the figure of Emma by her side, and Thackeray holding up Esmond. But no intelligent remark known to me will define the tract as a whole. All we can say of it is that it is bounded by two chains of mountains neither of which rises very abruptly – the opposing ranges of Poetry and of History – and bounded on the third side by a sea – a sea that we shall encounter when we come to *Moby Dick*.

In the first place, let us consider the proviso 'English Literature'. 'English' we shall of course interpret as written in English, not as published south of the Tweed or east of the Atlantic, or north of the Equator: we need not attend to geographical accidents, they can be left to the politicians. Yet,

1. *Le Roman Anglais de Notre Temps*, by Abel Chevalley (Milford, London).

even with this interpretation, are we as free as we wish? Can we, while discussing English fiction, quite ignore fiction written in other languages, particularly French and Russian? As far as influence goes, we could ignore it, for our writers have never been much influenced by the continentals. But – for reasons soon to be explained – I want to talk as little as possible about influence during these lectures. My subject is a particular kind of book and the aspects that book has assumed in English. Can we ignore its collateral aspects on the Continent? Not entirely. An unpleasant and unpatriotic truth has here to be faced. No English novelist is as great as Tolstoy – that is to say, has given so complete a picture of man's life, both on its domestic and heroic side. No English novelist has explored man's soul as deeply as Dostoyevsky. And no novelist anywhere has analysed the modern consciousness as successfully as Marcel Proust. Before these triumphs we must pause. English poetry fears no one – excels in quality as well as quantity. But English fiction is less triumphant: it does not contain the best stuff yet written, and if we deny this we become guilty of provincialism.

Now, provincialism does not signify in a writer, and may indeed be the chief source of his strength: only a prig or a fool would complain that Defoe is cockneyfied or Thomas Hardy countrified. But provincialism in a critic is a serious fault. A critic has no right to the narrowness which is the frequent prerogative of the creative artist. He has to have a wide outlook or he has not anything at all. Although the novel exercises the rights of a created object, criticism has not those rights, and too many little mansions in English fiction have been acclaimed to their own detriment as important edifices. Take four at random: *Cranford*, *The Heart of Midlothian*, *Jane Eyre*, *The Ordeal of Richard Feverel*. For various personal and local reasons we may be attached to these four books. *Cranford* radiates the humour of the urban midlands, *Midlothian* is a handful out of Edinburgh, *Jane Eyre* is the passionate dream of a fine but still undeveloped woman, *Richard Feverel* exudes farmhouse lyricism and flickers with modish wit. But all four are little mansions, not mighty edifices, and we shall see and respect them for what they are if we stand them for an instant in the colonnades of *War and Peace*, or the vaults of *The Brothers Karamazov*.

I shall not often refer to foreign novels in these lectures, still less would I pose as an expert on them who is debarred from discussing them by his terms of reference. But I do want to emphasize their greatness before we start; to cast, so to speak, this preliminary shadow over our subject, so that when we look back on it at the end we may have the better chance of seeing it in its true lights.

So much for the proviso 'English'. Now for a more important point, the proviso of 'period or periods'. This idea of a period or a development in time, with its consequent emphasis on influences and schools, happens to be exactly what I am hoping to avoid during our brief survey, and I believe that the author of *Gazpacho* will be lenient. Time, all the way through, is to be our enemy. We are to visualize the English novelists not as floating down that stream which bears all its sons away unless they are careful, but as seated together in a room, a circular room, a sort of British Museum reading-room – all writing their novels simultaneously. They do not, as they sit there, think: 'I live under Queen Victoria, I under Anne, I carry on the tradition of Trollope, I am reacting against Aldous Huxley.' The fact that their pens are in their hands is far more vivid to them. They are half mesmerized, their sorrows and joys are pouring out through the ink, they are approximated by the act of creation, and when Professor Oliver Elton says, as he does, that 'after 1847 the novel of passion was never to be the same again' none of them understands what he means. That is to be our vision of them – an imperfect vision, but it is suited to our powers, it will preserve us from a serious danger, the danger of pseudo-scholarship.

Genuine scholarship is one of the highest successes which our race can achieve. No one is more triumphant than the man who chooses a worthy subject and masters all its facts and the leading facts of the subjects neighbouring. He can then do what he likes. He can, if his subject is the novel, lecture on it chronologically if he wishes, because he has read all the important novels of the past four centuries, many of the unimportant ones, and has adequate knowledge of any collateral facts that bear upon English fiction. The late Sir Walter Raleigh (who once held this lectureship) was such a scholar. Raleigh knew so many facts that he was able to proceed to influences, and his monograph on the English novel adopts the treatment by period which his unworthy successor must avoid. The scholar, like the philosopher, can contemplate the river of time. He contemplates it not as a whole, but he can see the facts, the personalities, floating past him, and estimate the relations between them, and if his conclusions could be as valuable to us as they are to himself he would long ago have civilized the human race. As you know, he has failed. True scholarship is incommunicable, true scholars rare. There are a few scholars, actual or potential, in the audience today, but only a few, and there is certainly none on the platform. Most of us are pseudo-scholars, and I want to consider our characteristics with sympathy and respect, for we are a very large and quite a powerful class, eminent in Church and State, we control the education of the Empire, we lend to the Press such distinction as it consents to receive, and we are a welcome asset at dinner parties.

Pseudo-scholarship is, on its good side, the homage paid by ignorance to learning. It also has an economic side, on which we need not be hard. Most of us must get a job before thirty, or sponge on our relatives, and many jobs can only be got by passing an exam. The pseudo-scholar often does well in examinations (real scholars are not much good), and even when he fails he appreciates their innate majesty. They are gateways to employment, they have power to ban and bless. A paper on *King Lear* may lead somewhere, unlike the rather far-fetched play of the same name. It may be a stepping-stone to the Local Government Board. He does not often put it to himself openly and say: 'That's the use of knowing things, they help you to get on.' The economic pressure he feels is more often subconscious, and he goes to his exam merely feeling that a paper on *King Lear* is a tempestuous and terrible experience but an intensely real one. And whether he be cynical or naïve he is not to be blamed. As long as learning is connected with earning, as long as certain jobs can only be reached through exams, so long must we take the examination system seriously. If another ladder to employment was contrived, much so-called education would disappear, and no one be a penny the stupider.

It is when he comes to criticism – to a job like the present – that he can be so pernicious, because he follows the method of a true scholar without having his equipment. He classes books before he has understood or read them; that is his first crime. Classification by chronology. Books written before 1847, books written after it, books written after or before 1848. The novel in the reign of Queen Anne, the pre-novel, the *Ur*-novel, the novel of the future. Classification by subject-matter – sillier still. The literature of Inns, beginning with *Tom Jones*; the literature of the Women's Movement, beginning with *Shirley*; the literature of Desert Islands, from *Robinson Crusoe* to *The Blue Lagoon*; the literature of Rogues – dreariest of all, though the Open Road runs it pretty close; the literature of Sussex (perhaps the most devoted of the Home Counties); improper books – a serious though dreadful branch of enquiry, only to be pursued by pseudo-scholars of riper years; novels relating to industrialism, aviation, chiropody, the weather. I include the weather on the authority of the most amazing work on the novel that I have met for many years. It came over the Atlantic to me, nor shall I ever forget it. It was a literary manual entitled *Materials and Methods of Fiction*. The writer's name shall be concealed. He was a pseudo-scholar and a good one. He classified novels by their dates, their length, their locality, their sex, their point of view, till no more seemed possible. But he still had the weather up his sleeve, and when he brought it out it had nine heads. He gave an example under each head, for he was anything but slovenly, and we will run through his list. In the first place the weather can be 'decorative', as in Pierre Loti; then 'utilitarian' as in *The Mill on the Floss* (no Floss, no Mill; no Mill, no Tullivers); 'illustrative', as in *The Egoist*; 'planned in pre-established harmony', as by Fiona Macleod; 'in emotional contrast', as in *The Master of Ballantrae*; 'determinative of action', as in a certain Kipling story, where a man proposes to the wrong girl on account of a sandstorm; 'a controlling influence', *Richard Feverel*; 'itself a hero', like Vesuvius in *The Last Days of Pompeii*; and ninthly, it can be 'non-existent', as in a nursery tale. I liked him flinging in non-existence. It made everything so scientific and trim. But he himself remained a little dissatisfied, and having finished his classification he said yes, of course there was one more thing, and that was genius; it was useless for a novelist to know that there are nine sorts of weather, unless he had genius also. Cheered by this reflection, he classified novels by their tones. There are only two tones, personal and impersonal, and having given examples of each he grew pensive again and said: 'Yes, but you must have genius too, or neither tone will profit.'

This reference to genius is, again, typical of the pseudo-scholar. He loves mentioning genius, because the sound of the word exempts him from discovering its meaning. Literature is written by geniuses. Novelists are geniuses. There we are; now let us classify them. Which he does. Everything he says may be accurate but all is useless, because he is moving round books instead of through them, he either has not read them or cannot read them properly. Books have to be read (worse luck, for it takes a long time); it is the only way of discovering what they contain. A few savage tribes eat them, but reading is the only method of assimilation revealed to the West. The reader must sit down alone and struggle with the writer, and this the pseudo-scholar will not do. He would rather relate a book to the history of its time, to events in the life of its author, to the events it describes, above all to some tendency. As soon as he can use the word 'tendency' his spirits rise, and though those of his audience may sink they often pull out their pencils at this point and make a note, under the belief that a tendency is portable.

That is why, in the rather ramshackly course that lies ahead of us, we cannot consider fiction by periods, we must not contemplate the stream of time. Another image better suits our powers: that of all the novelists writing their novels at once. They come from different ages and ranks, they have different temperaments and aims, but they all hold pens in their hands, and are in the process of creation. Let us look over their shoulders for a moment and see what they are writing. It may exorcise that demon of chronology which is at present our enemy and which (we shall discover next week) is sometimes their enemy too. 'Oh, what quenchless feud is this, that Time hath with the sons of Men,' cries Herman Melville, and the feud goes on not only in life and death but in the byways of literary creation and criticism. Let us avoid it by imagining that all the novelists are at work together in a circular room. I shall not mention their names until we have heard their words, because a name brings associations with it, dates, gossip, all the furniture of the method we are discarding.

They have been instructed to group themselves in pairs. The first pair write as follows:

1. I don't know what to do, not I! – God forgive me, but I am very impatient! I wish – But I don't know what to wish, without a sin! – Yet I wish it would please God to take me to his mercy! – I can meet with none here – What a world is this! – What is there

in it desirable? The good we hope for, so strangely mixed, that one knows not what to wish for! And one half of mankind tormenting the other, and being tormented themselves in tormenting!

2. What I hate is myself – when I think that one has to take so much, to be happy, out of the lives of others, and that one isn't happy even then. One does it to cheat one's self and to stop one's mouth – but that is only, at the best, for a little. The wretched self is always there, always making us somehow a fresh anxiety. What it comes to is that it's not, that it's never, a happiness, any happiness at all, to *take*. The only safe thing is to give. It's what plays you least false.

It is obvious that here sit two novelists who are looking at life from much the same angle, yet the first of them is Samuel Richardson, and the second you will have already identified as Henry James. Each is an anxious rather than an ardent psychologist. Each is sensitive to suffering and appreciates self-sacrifice; each falls short of the tragic, though a close approach is made. A sort of tremulous nobility – that is the spirit that dominates them – and oh how well they write! – not a word out of place in their copious flows. A hundred and fifty years of time divide them, but are not they close together in other ways, and may not their neighbourliness profit us? Of course as I say this I hear Henry James beginning to express his regret – no, not his regret but his surprise – no, not even his surprise but his awareness that neighbourliness is being postulated of him, and postulated, must he add, in relation to a shopkeeper. And I hear Richardson, equally cautious, wondering whether any writer born outside England can be chaste. But these are surface differences, are indeed additional points of contact. We leave them sitting in harmony, and proceed to our next pair.

1. All the preparations for the funeral ran easily and happily under Mrs Johnson's skilful hands. On the eve of the sad occasion she produced a reserve of black sateen, the kitchen steps, and a box of tintacks, and decorated the house with festoons and bows

of black in the best possible taste. She tied up the knocker with black crepe, and put a large bow over the corner of the steel engraving of Garibaldi, and swathed the bust of Mr Gladstone that had belonged to the deceased with inky swathings. She turned the two vases that had views of Tivoli and the Bay of Naples round, so that these rather brilliant landscapes were hidden and only the plain blue enamel showed, and she anticipated the long contemplated purchase of a tablecloth for the front room, and substituted a violet purple cover for the now very worn and faded raptures and roses in plushette that had hitherto done duty there. Everything that loving consideration could do to impart a dignified solemnity to her little home was done.

2. The air of the parlour being faint with the smell of sweet cake, I looked about for the table of refreshments; it was scarcely visible until one had got accustomed to the gloom, but there was a cut-up plum-cake upon it, and there were cut-up oranges, and sandwiches, and biscuits, and two decanters that I knew very well as ornaments, but had never seen used in all my life: one full of port, and one of sherry. Standing at this table, I became conscious of the servile Pumblechook in a black cloak and several yards of hatband, who was alternately stuffing himself, and making obsequious movements to catch my attention. The moment he succeeded, he came over to me (breathing sherry and crumbs), and said in a subdued voice, 'May I, dear sir?' and did.

These two funerals did not happen on the same day. One is that of Mr Polly's father (1910), the other Mrs Gargery's in *Great Expectations* (1861). Yet Wells and Dickens have the same point of view and even use the same tricks of style (cf. the two vases and the two decanters). They are, both, humorists and visualizers who get an effect by cataloguing details and whisking the page over irritably. They are generous-minded; they hate shams and enjoy being indignant about them; they are valuable social reformers; they have no notion of confining books to a library shelf. Sometimes the lively surface of their prose scratches like a cheap gramophone record, a certain poorness of quality appears, and the face of the author draws rather too near to that of the reader. In other words, neither of them has much taste: the world of beauty was largely closed to Dickens, and is entirely closed to Wells. And there are other parallels – for instance their method of drawing character. And perhaps the main difference between them is the difference of opportunity offered to an obscure boy of genius a hundred years ago and forty years ago. The difference is in Wells's favour. He is better educated than his predecessor; in particular the addition of science has strengthened his mind and subdued his hysteria. He registers an improvement in society – Dotheboys Hall has been superseded by the Polytechnic – not any change in the novelist's art.

What about our next pair?

1. But for that mark, I'm not sure about it; I don't believe it was made by a nail after all; it's too big, too round, for that. I might get up, but if I got up and looked at it, ten to one I shouldn't be able to say for certain; because once a thing's done, no one ever knows how it happened. Oh! dear me, the mystery of life; the inaccuracy of thought! The ignorance of humanity! To show how very little control of our possessions we have – what an accidental affair this living is after all our civilization – let me just count over a few of the things lost in one lifetime, beginning, for that seems always the most mysterious of losses – what cat would gnaw, what rat would nibble – three pale blue canisters of bookbinding tools? Then there were the bird cages, the iron hoops, the steel skates, the Queen Anne coal-scuttle, the bagatelle board, the hand organ – all gone, and jewels, too. Opals and emeralds, they lie about the roots of turnips. What a scraping paring affair it is to be sure! The wonder is that I've any clothes on my back, that I sit surrounded by solid furniture at this moment. Why, if one wants to compare life to anything, one must liken it to being blown through the Tube at fifty miles an hour . . .

2. Every day for at least ten years together did my father resolve to have it mended – 'tis not mended yet; – no family but ours would have borne with it an hour – and what is most astonishing, there was not a subject in the world upon which my father

34

was so eloquent, as upon that of door-hinges. – And yet at the same time, he was certainly one of the greatest bubbles to them, I think, that history can produce: his rhetoric and conduct were at perpetual handy-cuffs. Never did the parlour-door open – but his philosophy or his principles fell a victim to it; – three drops of oil with a feather, and a smart stroke of a hammer, had saved his honour for ever.

– Inconsistent soul that man is! – languishing under wounds, which he has the power to heal! – his whole life a contradiction to his knowledge! – his reason, that precious gift of God to him – (instead of pouring in oil) serving but to sharpen his sensibilities – to multiply his pains, and render him more melancholy and uneasy under them! – Poor unhappy creature, that he should do so! – Are not the necessary causes of misery in this life enow, but he must add voluntary ones to his stock of sorrow; – struggle against evils which cannot be avoided, and submit to others, which a tenth part of the trouble they create him would remove from his heart for ever?

By all that is good and virtuous, if there are three drops of oil to be got, and a hammer to be found within ten miles of *Shandy Hall* – the parlour door hinge shall be mended this reign.

The passage last quoted is, of course, out of *Tristram Shandy*. The other passage was from Virginia Woolf. She and Sterne are both fantasists. They start with a little object, take a flutter from it, and settle on it again. They combine a humorous appreciation of the muddle of life with a keen sense of its beauty. There is even the same tone in their voices – a rather deliberate bewilderment, an announcement to all and sundry that they do not know where they are going. No doubt their scales of value are not the same. Sterne is a sentimentalist, Virginia Woolf (except perhaps in her latest work, *To the Lighthouse*) is extremely aloof. Nor are their achievements on the same scale. But their medium is similar, the same odd effects are obtained by it, the parlour door is never mended, the mark on the wall turns out to be a snail, life is such a muddle, oh dear, the will is so weak, the sensations fidgety . . .

philosophy . . . God . . . oh dear, look at the mark . . . listen to
the door – existence . . . is really too . . . what were we saying?

Does not chronology seem less important now that we have
visualized six novelists at their jobs? If the novel develops, is
it not likely to develop on different lines from the British
Constitution, or even the Women's Movement? I say 'even
the Women's Movement' because there happened to be a
close association between fiction in England and that movement during the nineteenth century – a connection so close
that it has misled some critics into thinking it an organic
connection. As women bettered their position the novel,
they asserted, became better too. Quite wrong. A mirror
does not develop because an historical pageant passes in
front of it. It only develops when it gets a fresh coat of quicksilver – in other words, when it acquires new sensitiveness;
and the novel's success lies in its own sensitiveness, not in the
success of its subject-matter. Empires fall, votes are accorded, but to those people writing in the circular room it is
the feel of the pen between their fingers that matters most.
They may decide to write a novel upon the French or the
Russian Revolution, but memories, associations, passions,
rise up and cloud their objectivity, so that at the close, when
they reread, someone else seems to have been holding their
pen and to have relegated their theme to the background.
That 'someone else' is their self no doubt, but not the self
that is so active in time and lives under George IV or V.
All through history writers while writing have felt more or
less the same. They have entered a common state which it
is convenient to call inspiration, [1] and, having regard to that
state, we may say that History develops, Art stands still.

History develops, Art stands still, is a crude motto, indeed
it is almost a slogan, and though forced to adopt it we must

1. I have touched on this theory of inspiration in a short essay called
Anonymity (published by the Hogarth Press).

not do so without admitting its vulgarity. It contains only a partial truth.

It debars us in the first place from considering whether the human mind alters from generation to generation; whether, for instance, Thomas Deloney, who wrote humorously about shops and pubs in the reign of Queen Elizabeth, differs fundamentally from his modern representative – who would be someone of the calibre of Neil Lyons or Pett Ridge. As a matter of fact I believe Deloney did not differ; differed as an individual, but not fundamentally, not because he lived four hundred years ago. Four thousand, fourteen thousand years, might give us pause, but four hundred years is nothing in the life of our race, and does not allow room for any measurable change. So our slogan here is no practical hindrance. We can chant it without shame.

It is more serious when we turn to the development of tradition and see what we lose through being debarred from examining that. Apart from schools and influences and fashions, there has been a technique in English fiction, and this does alter from generation to generation. The technique of laughing at characters for instance: to smoke and to rag are not identical; the Elizabethan humorist picks up his victim in a different way from the modern, raises his laugh by other tricks. Or the technique of fantasy: Virginia Woolf, though her aim and general effect both resemble Sterne's, differs from him in execution; she belongs to the same tradition but to a later phase of it. Or the technique of conversation: in my pairs of examples I could not include a couple of dialogues, for the reason that the use of the 'he said' and 'she said' varies so much through the centuries that it colours its surroundings, and though the speakers may be similarly conceived they will not seem so in an extract. Well, we cannot examine questions like these, and must admit we are the poorer, though we can abandon the development of subject-matter and the development of the

37

ASPECTS OF THE NOVEL

human race without regret. Literary tradition is the border-
land lying between literature and history, and the well-
equipped critic will spend much time there and enrich his
judgement accordingly. We cannot go there because we
have not read enough. We must pretend it belongs to history
and cut it off accordingly. We must refuse to have anything
to do with chronology.

Let me quote here for our comfort from my immediate
predecessor in this lectureship, Mr T. S. Eliot. Mr Eliot
enumerates, in the introduction to *The Sacred Wood*, the
duties of the critic:

> It is part of the business of the critic to preserve tradition – where
> a good tradition exists. It is part of his business to see literature
> steadily and to see it whole; and this is eminently to see it *not* as
> consecrated by time, but to see it beyond time...

The first duty we cannot perform, the second we must try
to perform. We can neither examine nor preserve tradition.
But we can visualize the novelists as sitting in one room,
and force them, by our very ignorance, from the limitations
of date and place. I think that is worth doing, or I should
not have ventured to undertake this course.

How then are we to attack the novel – that spongy tract,
those fictions in prose of a certain extent which extend so in-
determinately? Not with any elaborate apparatus. Principles and systems may suit other forms of art, but they cannot be applicable here – or if applied their results must be
subjected to re-examination. And who is the re-examiner?
Well, I am afraid it will be the human heart, it will be this
man-to-man business, justly suspect in its cruder forms. The
final test of a novel will be our affection for it, as it is the
test of our friends, and of anything else which we cannot
define. Sentimentality – to some a worse demon than
chronology – will lurk in the background saying, 'Oh, but
I like that,' 'Oh, but that doesn't appeal to me,' and all I

can promise is that sentimentality shall not speak too loudly or too soon. The intensely, stiflingly human quality of the novel is not to be avoided; the novel is sogged with humanity; there is no escaping the uplift or the downpour, nor can they be kept out of criticism. We may hate humanity, but if it is exorcised or even purified the novel wilts, little is left but a bunch of words.

And I have chosen the title *Aspects* because it is unscientific and vague, because it leaves us the maximum of freedom, because it means both the different ways we can look at a novel and the different ways a novelist can look at his work. And the aspects selected for discussion are seven in number: The Story; People; The Plot; Fantasy and Prophecy; Pattern and Rhythm.

2

THE STORY

WE shall all agree that the fundamental aspect of the novel is its story-telling aspect, but we shall voice our assent in different tones, and it is on the precise tone of voice we employ now that our subsequent conclusions will depend.

Let us listen to three voices. If you ask one type of man, 'What does a novel do?' he will reply placidly: 'Well – I don't know – it seems a funny sort of question to ask – a novel's a novel – well, I don't know – I suppose it kind of tells a story, so to speak.' He is quite good-tempered and vague, and probably driving a motor-bus at the same time and paying no more attention to literature than it merits. Another man, whom I visualize as on a golf-course, will be aggressive and brisk. He will reply: 'What does a novel do? Why, tell a story of course, and I've no use for it if it didn't. I like a story. Very bad taste on my part, no doubt, but I like a story. You can take your art, you can take your literature, you can take your music, but give me a good story. And I like a story to be a story, mind, and my wife's the same.' And a third man, he says in a sort of drooping regretful voice: 'Yes – oh dear yes – the novel tells a story.' I respect and admire the first speaker. I detest and fear the second. And the third is myself. Yes – oh dear yes – the novel tells a story. That is the fundamental aspect without which it could not exist. That is the highest factor common to all novels, and I wish that it was not so, that it could be something different – melody, or perception of the truth, not this low atavistic form.

For, the more we look at the story (the story that is a story, mind), the more we disentangle it from the finer growths that it supports, the less shall we find to admire. It runs like a backbone – or may I say a tapeworm, for its beginning and end are arbitrary. It is immensely old – goes back to neolithic times, perhaps to palaeolithic. Neanderthal man listened to stories, if one may judge by the shape of his skull. The primitive audience was an audience of shock-heads, gaping round the camp-fire, fatigued with contending against the mammoth or the woolly rhinoceros, and only kept awake by suspense. What would happen next? The novelist droned on, and as soon as the audience guessed what happened next they either fell asleep or killed him. We can estimate the dangers incurred when we think of the career of Scheherazade in somewhat later times. Scheherazade avoided her fate because she knew how to wield the weapon of suspense – the only literary tool that has any effect upon tyrants and savages. Great novelist though she was – exquisite in her descriptions, tolerant in her judgements, ingenious in her incidents, advanced in her morality, vivid in her delineations of character, expert in her knowledge of three oriental capitals – it was yet on none of these gifts that she relied when trying to save her life from her intolerable husband. They were but incidental. She only survived because she managed to keep the king wondering what would happen next. Each time she saw the sun rising she stopped in the middle of a sentence, and left him gaping. 'At this moment Scheherazade saw the morning appearing and, discreet, was silent.' This uninteresting little phrase is the backbone of the *One Thousand and One Nights*, the tapeworm by which they are tied together and the life of a most accomplished princess was preserved.

We are all like Scheherazade's husband, in that we want to know what happens next. That is universal and that is why the backbone of a novel has to be a story. Some of us want to know nothing else – there is nothing in us but primeval curiosity, and consequently our other literary judgements are ludicrous. And now the story can be defined. It is a narrative of events arranged in their time-sequence – dinner coming after breakfast, Tuesday after Monday, decay after death, and so on. Qua story, it can only have one merit: that of making the audience want to know what happens next. And conversely it can only have one fault: that of making the audience not want to know what happens next. These are the only two criticisms that can be made on the story that is a story. It is the lowest and simplest of literary organisms. Yet it is the highest factor common to all the very complicated organisms known as novels.

When we isolate the story like this from the nobler aspects through which it moves, and hold it out on the forceps – wriggling and interminable, the naked worm of time – it presents an appearance that is both unlovely and dull. But we have much to learn from it. Let us begin by considering it in connection with daily life.

Daily life is also full of the time-sense. We think one event occurs after or before another, the thought is often in our minds, and much of our talk and action proceeds on the assumption. Much of our talk and action, but not all; there seems something else in life besides time, something which may conveniently be called 'value', something which is measured not by minutes or hours, but by intensity, so that when we look at our past it does not stretch back evenly but piles up into a few notable pinnacles, and when we look at the future it seems sometimes a wall, sometimes a cloud, sometimes a sun, but never a chronological chart. Neither memory nor anticipation is much interested in Father Time, and all dreamers, artists and lovers are partially delivered from his tyranny; he can kill them, but he cannot secure their attention, and at the very moment of doom, when the clock collected in the tower its strength and struck, they may be looking the other way. So daily life, whatever it may be really, is practically composed of two

lives – the life in time and the life by values – and our conduct reveals a double allegiance. 'I only saw her for five
minutes, but it was worth it.' There you have both alle-
giances in a single sentence. And what the story does is to
narrate the life in time. And what the entire novel does – if
it is a good novel – is to include the life by values as well;
using devices hereafter to be examined. It, also, pays a
double allegiance. But in it, in the novel, the allegiance to
time is imperative: no novel could be written without it.
Whereas in daily life the allegiance may not be necessary:
we do not know, and the experience of certain mystics
suggests, indeed, that it is not necessary, and that we are
quite mistaken in supposing that Monday is followed by
Tuesday, or death by decay. It is always possible for you or
me in daily life to deny that time exists and act accordingly
even if we become unintelligible and are sent by our fellow
citizens to what they choose to call a lunatic-asylum. But it
is never possible for a novelist to deny time inside the fabric
of his novel: he must cling, however lightly, to the thread
of his story, he must touch the interminable tapeworm,
otherwise he becomes unintelligible, which, in his case, is a
blunder.

I am trying not to be philosophic about time, for it is (ex-
perts assure us) a most dangerous hobby for an outsider, far
more fatal than place; and quite eminent metaphysicians
have been dethroned through referring to it improperly. I
am only trying to explain that as I lecture now I hear that
clock ticking or do not hear it ticking, I retain or lose the
time-sense; whereas in a novel there is always a clock. The
author may dislike his clock. Emily Brontë in *Wuthering
Heights* tried to hide hers. Sterne, in *Tristram Shandy*, turned
his upside down. Marcel Proust, still more ingenious, kept
altering the hands, so that his hero was at the same period
entertaining a mistress to supper and playing ball with his
nurse in the park. All these devices are legitimate, but none

of them contravene our thesis: the basis of a novel is a story, and a story is a narrative of events arranged in time-sequence. (A story, by the way, is not the same as a plot. It may form the basis of one, but the plot is an organism of a higher type, and will be defined and discussed in a future lecture.)

Who shall tell us a story?

Sir Walter Scott of course.

Scott is a novelist over whom we shall violently divide. For my own part I do not care for him, and find it difficult to understand his continued reputation. His reputation in his day – that is easy to understand. There are important historical reasons for it, which we should discuss if our scheme was chronological. But when we fish him out of the river of time, and set him to write in that circular room with the other novelists, he presents a less impressive figure. He is seen to have a trivial mind and a heavy style. He cannot construct. He has neither artistic detachment nor passion, and how can a writer who is devoid of both create characters who will move us deeply? Artistic detachment – perhaps it is priggish to ask for that. But passion – surely passion is lowbrow enough, and think how all Scott's laborious mountains and scooped-out glens and carefully ruined abbeys call out for passion, passion, and how it is never there! If he had passion he would be a great writer – no amount of clumsiness or artificiality would matter then. But he only has a temperate heart and gentlemanly feelings, and an intelligent affection for the countryside; and this is not basis enough for great novels. And his in-tegrity – that is worse than nothing, for it was a purely moral and commercial integrity. It satisfied his highest needs and he never dreamt that another sort of loyalty exists.

His fame is due to two causes. In the first place, many of the elder generation had him read aloud to them when they were young; he is entangled with happy sentimental memories, with holidays in or residence in Scotland. They love him indeed for the same reason that I loved and still love *The Swiss Family Robinson*. I could lecture to you now on *The Swiss Family Robinson* and it would be a glowing lecture, because of the emotions felt in boyhood. When my brain decays entirely I shall not bother any more over great literature. I shall go back to the romantic shore where 'the ship struck with a frightful shock', emitting four demigods named Fritz, Ernest, Jack and little Franz, together with their father, their mother, and a cushion, which contained all the appliances necessary for a ten years' residence in the tropics. That is my eternal summer, that is what *The Swiss Family Robinson* means to me, and is not it all that Sir Walter Scott means to some of you? Is he really more than a reminder of early happiness? And until our brains do decay must not we put all this aside when we attempt to understand books?

In the second place, Scott's fame rests upon one genuine basis. He could tell a story. He had the primitive power of keeping the reader in suspense and playing on his curiosity. Let us paraphrase *The Antiquary* – not analyse it, analysis is the wrong method, but paraphrase. Then we shall see the story unrolling itself, and be able to study its simple devices.

THE ANTIQUARY

CHAPTER I

It was early on a fine summer's day, near the end of the eighteenth century, when a young man, of genteel appearance, journeying towards the north-east of Scotland, provided himself with a ticket in one of those public carriages which travel between Edinburgh and the Queensferry, at which place, as the name implies, and as is well known to all my northern readers, there is a passage-boat for crossing the Firth of Forth.

That is the first sentence – not an exciting sentence, but it gives us the time, the place, and a young man, it sets the story-teller's scene. We feel a moderate interest in what the young man will do next. His name is Lovel, and there is a mystery about him. He is the hero, or Scott would not call him genteel, and he is sure to make the heroine happy. He meets the Antiquary, Jonathan Oldbuck. They get into the coach, not too quickly, become acquainted, Lovel visits Oldbuck at his house. Near it they meet a new character, Edie Ochiltree. Scott is good at introducing fresh characters. He slides them in very naturally, and with a promising air. Edie Ochiltree promises a good deal. He is a beggar – no ordinary beggar, a romantic and reliable rogue, and will he not help to solve the mystery of which we saw the tip in Lovel? More introductions: to Sir Arthur Wardour (old family, bad manager); to his daughter Isabella (haughty), whom the hero loves unrequited; to Oldbuck's sister Miss Grizzel. Miss Grizzel is introduced with the same air of promise. As a matter of fact she is just a comic turn – she leads nowhere, and your story-teller is full of these turns. He need not hammer away all the time at cause and effect. He keeps just as well within the simple boundaries of his art if he says things that have no bearing on the development. The audience thinks they will develop, but the audience is shock-headed and tired and easily forgets. Unlike the weaver of plots, the story-teller profits by ragged ends. Miss Grizzel is a small example of a ragged end; for a big one I would refer to a novel that professes to be lean and tragic: *The Bride of Lammermoor*. Scott presents the Lord High Keeper in this book with great emphasis and with endless suggestions that the defects of his character will lead to the tragedy, while as a matter of fact the tragedy would occur in almost the same form if he did not exist – the only necessary ingredients in it being Edgar, Lucy, Lady Ashton and Bucklaw. Well, to return to *The Antiquary*, then there is a dinner, Oldbuck and Sir Arthur quarrel, Sir Arthur is offended and leaves with his daughter, and they walk back across the sands. The tide rises. Sir Arthur and Isabella are cut off, and are confronted by Edie Ochiltree. This is the first serious moment in the story and this is how the story-teller who is a story-teller handles it:

While they exchanged these words, they paused upon the highest ledge of rock to which they could attain; for it seemed that any further attempt to move forward could only serve to anticipate their fate. Here, then, they were to await the sure though slow progress of the raging element, something in the situation of the martyrs of the Early Church, who, exposed by heathen tyrants to be slain by wild beasts, were compelled for a time to witness the impatience and rage by which the animals were agitated, while awaiting the signal for undoing their grates and letting them loose upon the victims.

Yet even this fearful pause gave Isabella time to collect the powers of a mind naturally strong and courageous, and which rallied itself at this terrible juncture. 'Must we yield life,' she said, 'without a struggle? Is there no path, however dreadful, by which we could climb the crag, or at least attain some height above the tide, where we could remain till morning, or till help comes? They must be aware of our situation, and will raise the country to relieve us.'

Thus speaks the heroine, in accents which certainly chill the reader. Yet we want to know what happens next. The rocks are of cardboard, like those in my dear *Swiss Family*; the tempest is turned on with one hand while Scott scribbles away about Early Christians with the other; there is no sincerity, no sense of danger in the whole affair; it is all passionless, perfunctory, yet we do just want to know what happens next.

Why – Lovel rescues them. Yes; we ought to have thought of that; and what then?

Another ragged end. Lovel is put by the Antiquary to sleep in a haunted room, where he has a dream or vision of his host's ancestor, who says to him, 'Kunst macht Gunst,' words which he does not understand at the time, owing to his ignorance of German, and learns afterwards that they mean 'Skill wins Favour': he must pursue the siege of Isabella's heart. That is to say, the supernatural contributes nothing to the story. It is introduced with tapestries and storms, but only a copybook maxim results. The reader does not know this, though. When he hears 'Kunst macht Gunst' his attention reawakes ... then his attention is diverted to something else, and the time-sequence goes on.

Picnic in the ruins of St Ruth. Introduction of Douster-swivel, a wicked foreigner, who has involved Sir Arthur in mining schemes and whose superstitions are ridiculed because not of the genuine Border brand. Arrival of Hector McIntyre, the Antiquary's nephew, who suspects Lovel of being an impostor. The two fight a duel; Lovel, thinking he has killed his opponent, flies with Edie Ochiltree, who has turned up as usual. They hide in the ruins of St Ruth, where they watch Dousterswivel gulling Sir Arthur in a treasure-hunt. Lovel gets away on a boat and – out of sight, out of mind; we do not worry about him until he turns up again. Second treasure-hunt at St Ruth. Sir Arthur finds a hoard of silver. Third treasure-hunt. Dousterswivel is soundly cudgelled, and when he comes to himself sees the funeral rites of the old Countess of Glenallan, who is being buried there at midnight and with secrecy, that family being of the Romish persuasion.

Now the Glenallans are very important in the story, yet how casually they are introduced! They are hooked on to Dousterswivel in the most artless way. His pair of eyes happened to be handy, so Scott had a peep through them. And the reader by now is getting so docile under the succession of episodes that he just gapes, like a primitive cave-man. Now the Glenallan interest gets to work, the ruins of St Ruth are switched off, and we enter what may be called the 'pre-story', where two new characters intervene, and talk wildly and darkly about a sinful past. Their names are:

Elspeth Mucklebackit, a Sibyl of a fisherwoman, and Lord
Glenallan, son of the dead countess. Their dialogue is inter-
rupted by other events – by the arrest, trial and release of
Edie Ochiltree, by the death by drowning of another new
character, and by the humours of Hector McIntyre's con-
valescence at his uncle's house. But the gist is that Lord
Glenallan many years ago had married a lady called
Evelina Nevile, against his mother's wish, and had then
been given to understand that she was his half-sister. Mad-
dened with horror, he had left her before she gave birth to a
child. Elspeth, formerly his mother's servant, now explains
to him that Evelina was no relation to him, that she died in
childbirth – Elspeth and another woman attending – and
that the child disappeared. Lord Glenallan then goes to
consult the Antiquary, who, as a Justice of the Peace, knew
something of the events of the time, and who had also loved
Evelina. And what happens next? Sir Arthur Wardour's
goods are sold up, for Dousterswivel has ruined him. And
then? The French are reported to be landing. And then?
Lovel rides into the district leading the British troops. He
calls himself Major Nevile now. But even Major Nevile is
not his right name, for he is who but the lost child of Lord
Glenallan, he is none other than the legitimate heir to an
earldom. Partly through Elspeth Mucklebackit, partly
through her fellow servant whom he meets as a nun abroad,
partly through an uncle who has died, partly through Edie
Ochiltree, the truth has come out. There are indeed plenty
of reasons for the dénouement, but Scott is not interested in
reasons; he dumps them down without bothering to eluci-
date them; to make one thing happen after another is his
only serious aim. And then? Isabella Wardour relents and
marries the hero. And then? That is the end of the story.
We must not ask 'And then?' too often. If the time-
sequence is pursued one second too far it leads us into quite
another country.

The Antiquary is a book in which the life in time is celebrated instinctively by the novelist, and this must lead to
slackening of emotion and shallowness of judgement, and in
particular to that idiotic use of marriage as a finale. Time
can be celebrated consciously also, and we shall find an example of this in a very different sort of book, in a memorable
book: Arnold Bennett's *The Old Wives' Tale*. Time is the
real hero of *The Old Wives' Tale*. He is installed as the lord
of creation – excepting indeed of Mr Critchlow, whose
bizarre exemption only gives added force. Sophia and Constance are the children of Time from the instant we see them
romping with their mother's dresses; they are doomed to
decay with a completeness that is very rare in literature.
They are girls, Sophia runs away and marries, the mother
dies, Constance marries, her husband dies, Sophia's husband dies, Sophia dies, Constance dies, their old rheumatic
dog lumbers up to see whether anything remains in the
saucer. Our daily life in time is exactly this business of getting old which clogs the arteries of Sophia and Constance,
and the story that is a story and sounded so healthy and
stood no nonsense cannot sincerely lead to any conclusion
but the grave. It is an unsatisfactory conclusion. Of course
we grow old. But a great book must rest on something more
than an 'of course', and though *The Old Wives' Tale* is
strong, sincere, sad, it misses greatness.

What about *War and Peace*? That is certainly great, that
likewise emphasizes the effects of time and the waxing and
waning of a generation. Tolstoy, like Bennett, has the courage to show us people getting old – the partial decay of
Nicolay and Natasha is really more sinister than the complete decay of Constance and Sophia: more of our own
youth seems to have perished in it. Then why is *War and
Peace* not depressing? Probably because it has extended over
space as well as over time, and the sense of space until it
terrifies us is exhilarating, and leaves behind it an effect like

music. After one has read *War and Peace* for a bit, great
chords begin to sound, and we cannot say exactly what
struck them. They do not arise from the story, though Tolstoy is quite as interested in what comes next as Scott, and
quite as sincere as Bennett. They do not come from the
episodes nor yet from the characters. They come from the
immense area of Russia, over which episodes and characters
have been scattered, from the sum total of bridges and
frozen rivers, forests, roads, gardens, fields, which accumu-
late grandeur and sonority after we have passed them.
Many novelists have the feeling for place – Five Towns,
Auld Reekie and so on. Very few have the sense of space,
and the possession of it ranks high in Tolstoy's divine equipment. Space is the lord of *War and Peace*, not time.

A word in conclusion about the story as the repository of a
voice. It is the aspect of the novelist's work which asks to be
read out loud, which appeals not to the eye, like most prose,
but to the ear; having indeed this much in common with
oratory. It does not offer melody or cadence. For these,
strange as it may seem, the eye is sufficient; the eye, backed
by a mind that transmutes, can easily gather up the sounds of
a paragraph or dialogue when they have aesthetic value, and
refer them to our enjoyment – yes, can even telescope them
up so that we get them quicker than we should do if they were
recited, just as some people can look through a musical score
quicker than it can be rapped out on the piano. But the eye is
not equally quick at catching a voice. That opening sentence
of *The Antiquary* has no beauty of sound, yet we should lose
something if it was not read aloud. Our mind would com-
mune with Walter Scott's silently, and less profitably. The
story, besides saying one thing after another, adds something
because of its connection with a voice.

It does not add much. It does not give us anything as important as the author's personality. His personality – when
he has one – is conveyed through nobler agencies, such as the

characters or the plot or his comments on life. What the story does do in this particular capacity, all it can do, is to transform us from readers into listeners, to whom 'a' voice speaks, the voice of the tribal narrator, squatting in the middle of the cave, and saying one thing after another until the audience falls asleep among their offal and bones. The story is primitive, it reaches back to the origins of literature, before reading was discovered, and it appeals to what is primitive in us. That is why we are so unreasonable over the stories we like, and so ready to bully those who like something else. For instance, I am annoyed when people laugh at me for loving *The Swiss Family Robinson*, and I hope that I have annoyed some of you over Scott! You see what I mean. Intolerance is the atmosphere stories generate. The story is neither moral nor is it favourable to the understanding of the novel in its other aspects. If we want to do that we must come out of the cave.

We shall not come out of it yet, but observe already how that other life – the life by value – presses against the novel from all sides, how it is ready to fill and indeed distort it, offering it people, plots, fantasies, views of the universe, anything except this constant 'and then . . . and then', which is the sole contribution of our present enquiry. The life in time is so obviously base and inferior that the question naturally occurs: cannot the novelist abolish it from his work, even as the mystic asserts he has abolished it from his experience, and install its radiant alternative alone?

Well, there is one novelist who has tried to abolish time, and her failure is instructive: Gertrude Stein. Going much further than Emily Brontë, Sterne or Proust, Gertrude Stein has smashed up and pulverized her clock and scattered its fragments over the world like the limbs of Osiris, and she has done this not from naughtiness but from a noble motive: she has hoped to emancipate fiction from the tyranny of time and to express in it the life by values only. She fails, because as soon as fiction is completely delivered from time it cannot express anything at all, and in her later writing we can see the slope down which she is slipping. She wants to abolish this whole aspect of the story, this sequence in chronology, and my heart goes out to her. She cannot do it without abolishing the sequence between the sentences. But this is not effective unless the order of the words in the sentences is also abolished, which in its turn entails the abolition of the order of the letters or sounds in the words. And now she is over the precipice. There is nothing to ridicule in such an experiment as hers. It is much more important to play about like this than to rewrite the Waverley Novels. Yet the experiment is doomed to failure. The time-sequence cannot be destroyed without carrying in its ruin all that should have taken its place; the novel that would express values only becomes unintelligible and therefore valueless.

That is why I must ask you to join me in repeating in exactly the right tone of voice the words with which this lecture opened. Do not say them vaguely and good-temperedly like a busman; you have not the right. Do not say them briskly and aggressively like a golfer; you know better. Say them a little sadly, and you will be correct. Yes – oh dear yes – the novel tells a story.

3

PEOPLE

HAVING discussed the story – that simple and fundamental aspect of the novel – we can turn to a more interesting topic: the actors. We need not ask what happened next, but to whom did it happen; the novelist will be appealing to our intelligence and imagination, not merely to our curiosity. A new emphasis enters his voice: emphasis upon value.

Since the actors in a story are usually human, it seemed convenient to entitle this aspect People. Other animals have been introduced, but with limited success, for we know too little so far about their psychology. There may be, probably will be, an alteration here in the future, comparable to the alteration in the novelist's rendering of savages in the past. The gulf that separates Man Friday from Batouala may be paralleled by the gulf that will separate Kipling's wolves from their literary descendants two hundred years hence, and we shall have animals who are neither symbolic, nor little men disguised, nor as four-legged tables moving, nor as painted scraps of paper that fly. It is one of the ways where science may enlarge the novel, by giving it fresh subject-matter. But the help has not been given yet, and until it comes we may say that the actors in a story are, or pretend to be, human beings.

Since the novelist is himself a human being, there is an affinity between him and his subject-matter which is absent in many other forms of art. The historian is also linked, though as we shall see, less intimately. The painter and sculptor need not be linked: that is to say, they need not represent human beings unless they wish, no more need the poet, while the musician cannot represent them even if he wishes, without the help of a programme. The novelist, unlike many of his colleagues, makes up a number of word-masses roughly describing himself (roughly: niceties shall come later), gives them names and sex, assigns them plausible gestures, and causes them to speak by the use of inverted commas, and perhaps to behave consistently. These word-masses are his characters. They do not come thus coldly to his mind, they may be created in delirious excitement, still, their nature is conditioned by what he guesses about other people, and about himself, and is further modified by the other aspects of his work. This last point – the relation of characters to the other aspects of the novel – will form the subject of a future enquiry. At present we are occupied with their relation to actual life. What is the difference between people in a novel and people like the novelist or like you, or like me, or Queen Victoria?

There is bound to be a difference. If a character in a novel is exactly like Queen Victoria – not rather like but exactly like – then it actually is Queen Victoria, and the novel, or all of it that the character touches, becomes a memoir. A memoir is history, it is based on evidence. A novel is based on evidence $+$ or $-x$, the unknown quantity being the temperament of the novelist; and the unknown quantity always modifies the effect of the evidence, and sometimes transforms it entirely.

The historian deals with actions, and with the characters of men only so far as he can deduce them from their actions. He is quite as much concerned with character as the novelist, but he can only know of its existence when it shows on the surface. If Queen Victoria had not said, 'We are not amused,' her neighbours at table would not have known she was not amused, and her ennui could never have been announced to the public. She might have frowned, so that they would have deduced her state from that – looks and gestures are also historical evidence. But if she remained impassive – what would anyone know? The hidden life is, by definition, hidden. The hidden life that appears in external signs is hidden no longer, has entered the realm of action. And it is the function of the novelist to reveal the hidden life at its source: to tell us more about Queen Victoria than could be known, and thus to produce a character who is not the Queen Victoria of history.

The interesting and sensitive French critic who writes under the name of Alain has some helpful if slightly fantastic remarks on this point. He gets a little out of his depth, but not as much as I feel myself out of mine, and perhaps together we may move towards the shore. Alain examines in his turn the various forms of aesthetic activity, and coming in time to the novel (*le roman*) he asserts that each human being has two sides, appropriate to history and fiction. All that is observable in a man – that is to say, his actions and such of his spiritual existence as can be deduced from his actions – falls into the domain of history. But his romanceful or romantic side (*sa partie romanesque ou romantique*) includes 'the pure passions, that is to say, the dreams, joys, sorrows and self-communings which politeness or shame prevent him from mentioning'; and to express this side of human nature is one of the chief functions of the novel.

What is fictitious in a novel is not so much the story as the method by which thought develops into action, a method which never occurs in daily life . . . History, with its emphasis on external causes, is dominated by the notion of fatality, whereas there is no fatality in the novel; there, everything is founded on human nature, and the dominating feeling is of an existence where everything is intentional, even passions and crimes, even misery.[1]

This is perhaps a roundabout way of saying what every British schoolboy knew, that the historian records whereas the novelist must create. Still, it is a profitable roundabout, for it brings out the fundamental difference between people in daily life and people in books. In daily life we never understand each other, neither complete clairvoyance nor complete

1. Paraphrased from *Système des Beaux Arts*, pp. 320–21. I am indebted to M. André Maurois for introducing me to this stimulating essay.

confessional exists. We know each other approximately, by external signs, and these serve well enough as a basis for society and even for intimacy. But people in a novel can be understood completely by the reader, if the novelist wishes; their inner as well as their outer life can be exposed. And this is why they often seem more definite than characters in history, or even our own friends; we have been told all about them that can be told; even if they are imperfect or unreal they do not contain any secrets, whereas our friends do and must, mutual secrecy being one of the conditions of life upon this globe.

Now let us re-state the problem in a more schoolboyish way. You and I are people. Had not we better glance through the main facts in our own lives – not in our individual careers but in our make-up as human beings? Then we shall have something definite to start from.

The main facts in human life are five: birth, food, sleep, love and death. One could increase the number – add breathing for instance – but these five are the most obvious. Let us briefly ask ourselves what part they play in our lives, and what in novels. Does the novelist tend to reproduce them accurately or does he tend to exaggerate, minimize, ignore, and to exhibit his characters going through processes which are not the same through which you and I go, though they bear the same names?

To consider the two strangest first: birth and death; strange because they are at the same time experiences and not experiences. We only know of them by report. We were all born, but we cannot remember what it was like. And death is coming even as birth has come, but, similarly, we do not know what it is like. Our final experience, like our first, is conjectural. We move between two darknesses. Certain people pretend to tell us what birth and death are like: a mother, for instance, has her point of view about birth; a doctor, a religious, have their points of view about both. But it is all from the outside, and the two entities who might enlighten us, the baby and the corpse, cannot do so, because their apparatus for communicating their experiences is not attuned to our apparatus for reception.

So let us think of people as starting life with an experience they forget and ending it with one which they anticipate but cannot understand. These are the creatures whom the novelist proposes to introduce as characters into books; these, or creatures plausibly like them. The novelist is allowed to remember and understand everything, if it suits him. He knows all the hidden life. How soon will he pick up his characters after birth, how close to the grave will he follow them? And what will he say, or cause to be felt, about these two queer experiences?

Then food, the stoking-up process, the keeping alive of an individual flame, the process that begins before birth and is continued after it by the mother, and finally taken over by the individual himself, who goes on day after day putting an assortment of objects into a hole in his face without becoming surprised or bored: food is a link between the known and the forgotten; closely connected with birth, which none of us remembers, and coming down to this morning's breakfast. Like sleep – which in many ways it resembles – food does not merely restore our strength, it has also an aesthetic side, it can taste good or bad. What will happen to this double-faced commodity in books?

And fourthly, sleep. On the average, about a third of our time is not spent in society or civilization or even in what is usually called solitude. We enter a world of which little is known and which seems to us after leaving it to have been partly oblivion, partly a caricature of this world and partly a revelation. 'I dreamt of nothing' or 'I dreamt of a ladder' or 'I dreamt of heaven,' we say when we wake. I do not want to discuss the nature of sleep and dreams – only to point out that they occupy much time and that what is called 'History' only busies itself with about two-thirds of the human cycle, and theorizes accordingly. Does fiction take up a similar attitude?

And lastly, love. I am using this celebrated word in its widest and dullest sense. Let me be very dry and brief about sex in the first place. Some years after a human being is born, certain changes occur in it, as in other animals, which changes often lead to union with another human being, and to the production of more human beings. And our race goes on. Sex begins before adolescence, and survives sterility; it is indeed coeval with our lives, although at the mating age its effects are more obvious to society. And besides sex there are other emotions, also strengthening towards maturity: the various upliftings of the spirit, such as affection, friendship, patriotism, mysticism – and as soon as we try to determine the relation between sex and these other emotions we shall of course begin to quarrel as violently as we ever could about Walter Scott, perhaps even more violently. Let me only tabulate the various points of view. Some people say that sex is basic and underlies all these other loves – love of friends, of God, of country. Others say that it is connected with them, but laterally, it is not their root. Others say that it is not connected at all. All I suggest is that we call the whole bundle of emotions love, and regard them as the fifth great experience through which human beings have to pass. When human beings love they try to get something. They also try to give something, and this double aim makes love more complicated than food or sleep. It is selfish and altruistic at the same time, and no amount of specialization in one direction quite atrophies the other. How much time does love take? This question sounds gross but it bears on our present enquiry. Sleep takes about eight hours out of the twenty-four, food about two more. Shall we put down love for another two? Surely that is a handsome allowance. Love may weave itself into our other activities – so may drowsiness and hunger. Love may start various secondary activities: for instance, a man's love for his family may cause him to spend a good deal of time on the Stock Exchange, or his love for God a good deal of time in church. But that he has emotional communion with any beloved object for more than two hours a day may be gravely doubted, and it is this emotional communion, this desire to give and to get, this mixture of generosity and expectation, that distinguishes love from the other experiences on our list.

That is the human make-up – or part of it. Made up like this himself, the novelist takes his pen in his hand, gets into the abnormal state which it is convenient to call 'inspiration', and tries to create characters. Perhaps the characters have to fall in with something else in his novel; this often happens (the books of Henry James are an extreme case), and then the characters have, of course, to modify the make-up accordingly. However, we are considering now the more simple case of the novelist whose main passion is human beings and who will sacrifice a great deal to their convenience – story, plot, form, incidental beauty.

Well, in what senses do the nations of fiction differ from those of the earth? One cannot generalize about them, because they have nothing in common in the scientific sense; they need not have glands, for example, whereas all human beings have glands. Nevertheless, though incapable of strict definition, they tend to behave along the same lines.

In the first place, they come into the world more like parcels than human beings. When a baby arrives in a novel it usually has the air of having been posted. It is delivered 'off'; one of the elder characters goes and picks it up and shows it to the reader, after which it is usually laid in cold storage until it can talk or otherwise assist in the action. There is both a good and a bad reason for this and for all other deviations from earthly practice; these we will note in a minute, but do just observe in what a very perfunctory way the population of noveldom is recruited. Between Sterne and James Joyce, scarcely any writer has tried either to use the facts of birth or to invent a new set of facts, and no one, except in a sort of auntish wistful way, has tried to work back towards the psychology of the baby's mind and to utilize the literary wealth that must lie there. Perhaps it cannot be done. We shall decide in a moment.

Death. The treatment of death, on the other hand, is nourished much more on observation, and has a variety about it which suggests that the novelist finds it congenial. He does, for the reason that death ends a book neatly, and for the less obvious reason that working as he does in time he finds it easier to work from the known towards the darkness rather than from the darkness of birth towards the known. By the time his characters die, he understands them, he can be both appropriate and imaginative about them – strongest of combinations. Take a little death – the death of Mrs Proudie in *The Last Chronicle of Barset*. All is in keeping, yet the effect is terrifying, because Trollope has ambled Mrs Proudie down many a diocesan bypath, showing her paces, making her snap, accustoming us, even to boredom, to her character and tricks, to her 'Bishop, consider the souls of the people', and then she has a heart-attack by the edge of her bed, she has ambled far enough – end of Mrs Proudie. There is scarcely anything that the novelist cannot borrow from 'daily death'; scarcely anything he may not profitably invent. The doors of that darkness lie open to him and he can even follow his characters through it, provided he is shod with imagination and does not try to bring us back scraps of séance information about the 'life beyond'.

What of food, the third fact upon our list? Food in fiction is mainly social. It draws characters together, but they seldom require it physiologically, seldom enjoy it, and never digest it unless specially asked to do so. They hunger for each other, as we do in life, but our equally constant longing for breakfast and lunch does not get reflected. Even poetry has made more of it – at least of its aesthetic side. Milton and Keats have both come nearer to the sensuousness of swallowing than George Meredith.

Sleep. Also perfunctory. No attempt to indicate oblivion or the actual dream-world. Dreams are either logical or else mosaics made out of hard little fragments of the past and future. They are introduced with a purpose, and that purpose is not the character's life as a whole, but that part of it he lives while awake. He is never conceived as a creature, a third of whose time is spent in the darkness. It is the limited daylight vision of the historian, which the novelist elsewhere avoids. Why should he not understand or reconstruct sleep? For remember, he has the right to invent, and we know when he is inventing truly, because his passion floats us over improbabilities. Yet he has neither copied sleep nor created it. It is just an amalgam.

Love. You all know how enormously love bulks in novels, and will probably agree with me that it has done them harm and made them monotonous. Why has this particular experience, especially in its sex form, been transplanted in such generous quantities? If you think of a novel in the vague you think of a love interest – of a man and woman who want to be united and perhaps succeed. If you think of your own life in the vague, or of a group of lives, you are left with a very different and a more complex impression.

There would seem to be two reasons why love, even in good novels, is so prominent.

Firstly, when the novelist ceases to design his characters and begins to create them, 'love' in any or all of its aspects becomes important in his mind, and without intending to do so he makes his characters unduly sensitive to it – unduly in the sense that they would not trouble so much in life. The constant sensitiveness of characters for each other – even in writers called robust like Fielding – is remarkable, and has no parallel in life, except among people who have plenty of leisure. Passion, intensity at moments – yes, but not this constant awareness, this endless readjusting, this ceaseless hunger. I believe that these are the reflections of the novelist's own state of mind while he composes, and that the predominance of love in novels is partly because of this.

A second reason; which logically comes into another part of our enquiry, but it shall be noted here. Love, like death, is congenial to a novelist because it ends a book conveniently. He can make it a permanency, and his readers easily acquiesce, because one of the illusions attached to love is that it will be permanent. Not has been – will be. All history, all our experience, teaches us that no human relationship is constant, it is as unstable as the living beings who compose it, and they must balance like jugglers if it is to remain; if it is constant it is no longer a human relationship but a social habit, the emphasis in it has passed from love to marriage. All this we know, yet we cannot bear to apply our bitter knowledge to the future; the future is to be so different; the perfect person is to come along, or the person we know already is to become perfect. There are to be no changes, no necessity for alertness. We are to be happy or even perhaps miserable for ever and ever. Any strong emotion brings with it the illusion of permanence, and the novelists have seized upon this. They usually end their books with marriage, and we do not object because we lend them our dreams.

Here we must conclude our comparison of those two allied species, Homo Sapiens and Homo Fictus. Homo Fictus is more elusive than his cousin. He is created in the minds of hundreds of different novelists, who have conflicting methods of gestation, so one must not generalize. Still, one can say a little about him. He is generally born off, he is capable of dying on, he wants little food or sleep, he is tirelessly occupied with human relationships. And – most important – we can know more about him than we can know about any of our fellow creatures, because his creator and narrator are one. Were we equipped for hyperbole, we might exclaim at this point: 'If God could tell the story of the universe, the universe would become fictitious.' For this is the principle involved.

Let us, after these high speculations, take an easy character and study it for a little. Moll Flanders will do.[1] She fills the book that bears her name, or rather stands alone in it, like a tree in a park, so that we can see her from every aspect and are not bothered by rival growths. Defoe is telling a story, like Scott, and we shall find stray threads left about in much the same way, on the chance of the writer wanting to pick them up afterwards: Moll's early batch of children for instance. But the parallel between Scott and Defoe cannot be pressed. What interested Defoe was the heroine, and the form of his book proceeds naturally out of her character. Seduced by a younger brother and married to an elder, she takes to husbands in the earlier and brighter part of her career; not to prostitution, which she detests with all the force of a decent and affectionate heart. She and most of the characters in Defoe's underworld are kind to one another, they save each other's feelings and run risks through personal loyalty. Their innate goodness is always flourishing despite the author's better judgement, the reason evidently being that the author had some great experience himself while in Newgate. We do not know what it was, probably he himself did not know afterwards, for he was a busy slipshod journalist and a keen politician. But something occurred to him in prison, and out of its vague, powerful emotion Moll and Roxana are born. Moll is a character physically, with hard plump limbs that get into bed and pick pockets. She lays no stress upon her appearance, yet she moves us as having height and weight, as breathing and

1. There are convenient reprints of *Moll Flanders* and *Roxana* in the Abbey Classics (Simpkin, Marshall & Co.). [In 1975 both novels were available in the Oxford English Novels; *Moll Flanders* also in Signet Books (New American Library) and Everyman's Library (Dent).]

eating, and doing many of the things that are usually
missed out. Husbands were her earlier employ: she was
trigamous if not quadrigamous, and one of her husbands
turned out to be a brother. She was happy with all of them,
they were nice to her, she nice to them. Listen to the pleasant jaunt her draper husband took her:

'Come, my dear,' says he to me one day, 'shall we go and take a
turn into the country for about a week?' 'Ay, my dear,' says I,
'whither would you go?' 'I care not whither,' says he, 'but I have
a mind to look like quality for a week. We'll go to Oxford,' says
he. 'How,' says I, 'shall we go? I am no horsewoman, and 'tis too
far for a coach.' 'Too far!' says he; 'no place is too far for a coach-
and-six. If I carry you out, you shall travel like a duchess.' 'Hum,'
says I, 'my dear, 'tis a frolic; but if you have a mind to it, I don't
care.' Well, the time was appointed, we had a rich coach, very
good horses, a coachman, postilion, and two footmen in very
good liveries; a gentleman on horseback, and a page with a
feather in his hat upon another horse. The servants all called him
my lord, and the inn-keepers, you may be sure, did the like, and
I was her honour the Countess, and thus we travelled to Oxford,
and a very pleasant journey we had; for, give him his due, not a
beggar alive knew better how to be a lord than my husband. We
saw all the rarities at Oxford, talked with two or three Fellows of
colleges about putting out a young nephew, that was left to his
lordship's care, to the University, and of their being his tutors.
We diverted ourselves with bantering several other poor scholars,
with hopes of being at least his lordship's chaplains and putting
on a scarf; and thus having lived like quality indeed, as to expense,
we went away for Northampton, and, in a word, in about twelve
days' ramble came home again, to the tune of about £93 expense.

Contrast with this the scene with her Lancashire husband,
whom she deeply loved. He is a highwayman, and each by
pretending to wealth has trapped the other into marriage.
After the ceremony, they are mutually unmasked, and if
Defoe were writing mechanically he would set them to up-
braid one another, like Mr and Mrs Lammle in *Our Mutual*

Friend. But he has given himself over to the humour and good sense of his heroine.

'Truly,' said I to him, 'I found you would soon have conquered me; and it is my affliction now, that I am not in a condition to let you see how easily I should have been reconciled to you, and have passed by all the tricks you had put upon me, in recompense of so much good-humour. But, my dear,' said I, 'what can we do now? We are both undone, and what better are we for our being reconciled together, seeing we have nothing to live on?'

We proposed a great many things, but nothing could offer where there was nothing to begin with. He begged me at last to talk no more of it, for, he said, I would break his heart; so we talked of other things a little, till at last he took a husband's leave of me, and so we went to sleep.

Which is both truer to daily life and pleasanter to read than Dickens. The couple are up against facts, not against the author's theory of morality, and being sensible good-hearted rogues they make no fuss. In the later part of her career she turns from husbands to thieving; she thinks this a change for the worse and a natural darkness spreads over the scene. But she is as firm and amusing as ever. How just are her reflections when she robs of her gold necklace the little girl returning from the dancing-class! The deed is done in the little passage leading to St Bartholomew's, Smithfield (you can visit the place today – Defoe haunts London), and her impulse is to kill the child as well. She does not, the impulse is very feeble, but conscious of the risk the child has run she becomes indignant with the parents for 'leaving the poor little lamb to come home by itself, and it would teach them to take more care of it another time'. How heavily and pretentiously a modern psychologist would labour to express this! It just runs off Defoe's pen, and so in another passage, where Moll cheats a man, and then tells him pleasantly afterwards that she has done so, with the result that she slides still further into his good graces, and cannot bear to cheat him any more. Whatever she does gives us a slight shock – not the jolt of disillusionment, but the thrill that proceeds from a living being. We laugh at her, but without bitterness or superiority. She is neither hypocrite nor fool.

Towards the end of the book she is caught in a draper's shop by two young ladies from behind the counter: 'I would have given them good words, but there was no room for it: two fiery dragons could not have been more furious than they were' – they call for the police, she is arrested and sentenced to death and then transported to Virginia instead. The clouds of misfortune lift with indecent rapidity. The voyage is a very pleasant one, owing to the kindness of the old woman who had originally taught her to steal. And (better still) her Lancashire husband happens to be transported also. They land at Virginia where, much to her distress, her brother-husband proves to be in residence. She conceals this, he dies, and the Lancashire husband only blames her for concealing it from him; he has no other grievance, for the reason that he and she are still in love. So the book closes prosperously, and firm as at the opening sentence the heroine's voice rings out: '... we resolve to spend the remainder of our years in sincere penitence for the wicked lives we have lived.'

Her penitence is sincere, and only a superficial judge will condemn her as a hypocrite. A nature such as hers cannot for long distinguish between doing wrong and getting caught – for a sentence or two she disentangles them but they insist on blending, and that is why her outlook is so cockneyfied and natural, with 'sich is life' for a philosophy and Newgate in the place of Hell. If we were to press her or her creator Defoe and say, 'Come, be serious. Do you believe in Infinity?' they would say (in the parlance of their modern descendants), 'Of course I believe in Infinity – what do you take me for?' – a confession of faith that slams the door on Infinity more completely than could any denial.

Moll Flanders, then, shall stand as our example of a novel in which a character is everything and is given freest play. Defoe makes a slight attempt at a plot with the brother-husband as a centre, but he is quite perfunctory, and her legal husband (the one who took her on the jaunt to Oxford) just disappears and is heard of no more. Nothing matters but the heroine; she stands in an open space like a tree, and, having said that she seems absolutely real from every point of view, we must ask ourselves whether we should recognize her if we met her in daily life. For that is the point we are still considering: the difference between people in life and people in books. And the odd thing is, that even though we take a character as natural and un-theoretical as Moll, who would coincide with daily life in every detail, we should not find her there as a whole. Suppose I suddenly altered my voice from a lecturing voice into an ordinary one and said to you, 'Look out – I can see Moll in the audience – look out, Mr' – naming one of you by name – 'she as near as could be got your watch' – well, you would know at once that I was wrong, that I was sinning not only against probabilities, which does not signify, but against daily life and books and the gulf that divides them. If I said, 'Look out, there's someone like Moll in the audience,' you might not believe me but you would not be annoyed by my imbecile lack of taste: I should only be sinning against probability. To suggest that Moll is in Cambridge this afternoon or anywhere in England, or has been anywhere in England, is idiotic. Why?

This particular question will be easy to answer next week, when we shall deal with more complicated novels, where the character has to fit in with other aspects of fiction. We shall then be able to make the usual reply, which we find in all manuals of literature, and which should always be given in an examination paper, the aesthetic reply, to the effect that a novel is a work of art, with its own laws, which are not those of daily life, and that a character in a novel is real when it lives in accordance with such laws. Amelia or Emma, we shall then say, cannot be at this lecture because they exist only in the books called after them, only in worlds of Fielding or Jane Austen. The barrier of art divides them from us. They are real not because they are like ourselves (though they may be like us) but because they are convincing.

It is a good answer, it will lead on to some sound conclusions. Yet it is not satisfactory for a novel like *Moll Flanders*, where the character is everything and can do what it likes. We want a reply that is less aesthetic and more psychological. Why cannot she be here? What separates her from us? Our answer has already been implied in that quotation from Alain: she cannot be here because she belongs to a world where the secret life is visible, to a world that is not and cannot be ours, to a world where the narrator and the creator are one. And now we can get a definition as to when a character in a book is real: it is real when the novelist knows everything about it. He may not choose to tell us all he knows – many of the facts, even of the kind we call obvious, may be hidden. But he will give us the feeling that though the character has not been explained it is explicable, and we get from this a reality of a kind we can never get in daily life.

For human intercourse, as soon as we look at it for its own sake and not as a social adjunct, is seen to be haunted by a spectre. We cannot understand each other, except in a rough and ready way; we cannot reveal ourselves, even when we want to; what we call intimacy is only a makeshift; perfect knowledge is an illusion. But in the novel we can know people perfectly, and, apart from the general pleasure of reading, we can find here a compensation for their dimness in life. In this direction fiction is truer than history, because it goes beyond the evidence, and each of us knows from his own experience that there is something beyond the evidence, and, even if the novelist has not got it correctly, well – he has tried. He can post his people in as babies, he can cause them to go on without sleep or food, he can make them be in love, love and nothing but love, provided he seems to know everything about them, provided they are his creations. That is why Moll Flanders cannot be here, that is one of the reasons why Amelia and Emma cannot be here. They are people whose secret lives are visible or might be visible; we are people whose secret lives are invisible.

And that is why novels, even when they are about wicked people, can solace us: they suggest a more comprehensible and thus a more manageable human race, they give us the illusion of perspicacity and of power.

4

PEOPLE
(CONTINUED)

WE now turn from transplantation to acclimatization. We
have discussed whether people could be taken out of life and
put into a book, and conversely whether they could come
out of books and sit down in this room. The answer suggested was in the negative and led to a more vital question:
can we, in daily life, understand each other? Today our
problems are more academic. We are concerned with the
characters in their relation to other aspects of the novel: to
a plot, a moral, their fellow characters, atmosphere, etc.
They will have to adapt themselves to other requirements
of their creator.

It follows that we shall no longer expect them to coincide
as a whole with daily life, only to parallel it. When we say
that a character in Jane Austen, Miss Bates for instance, is
'so like life' we mean that each bit of her coincides with a
bit of life, but that she as a whole only parallels the chatty
spinster we met at tea. Miss Bates is bound by a hundred
threads to Highbury. We cannot tear her away without
bringing her mother too, and Jane Fairfax and Frank Chur-
chill, and the whole of Box Hill; whereas we could tear
Moll Flanders away, at least for the purposes of experiment.
A Jane Austen novel is more complicated than a Defoe, because the characters are interdependent, and there is the
additional complication of a plot. The plot in *Emma* is not
prominent and Miss Bates contributes little. Still, it is there,
she is connected with the principals, and the result is a
closely woven fabric from which nothing can be removed.
Miss Bates and Emma herself are like bushes in a shrubbery
– not isolated trees like Moll – and anyone who has tried to

thin out a shrubbery knows how wretched the bushes look if they are transplanted elsewhere, and how wretched is the look of the bushes that remain. In most books the characters cannot spread themselves. They must exercise a mutual restraint.

The novelist, we are beginning to see, has a very mixed lot of ingredients to handle. There is the story, with its time-sequence of 'and then ... and then ...'; there are ninepins about whom he might tell the story, and tell a rattling good one, but no, he prefers to tell his story about human beings; he takes over the life by values as well as the life in time. The characters arrive when evoked, but full of the spirit of mutiny. For they have these numerous parallels with people like ourselves, they try to live their own lives and are consequently often engaged in treason against the main scheme of the book. They 'run away', they 'get out of hand'; they are creations inside a creation, and often inharmonious towards it; if they are given complete freedom they kick the book to pieces, and if they are kept too sternly in check they revenge themselves by dying, and destroy it by intestinal decay.

These trials beset the dramatist also, and he has yet another set of ingredients to cope with – the actors and actresses – and they appear to side sometimes with the characters they represent, sometimes with the play as a whole, and more often to be the mortal enemies of both. The weight they throw is incalculable, and how any work of art survives their arrival I do not understand. Concerned with a lower form of art, we need not worry – but, in passing, is it not extraordinary that plays on the stage are often better than they are in the study, and that the introduction of a bunch of rather ambitious and nervous men and women should add anything to our understanding of Shakespeare and Chekhov?

No, the novelist has difficulties enough, and today we

shall examine two of his devices for solving them – instinctive devices, for his methods when working are seldom the same as the methods we use when examining his work. The first device is the use of different kinds of characters. The second is connected with the point of view.

I

We may divide characters into flat and round.

Flat characters were called 'humours' in the seventeenth century, and are sometimes called types, and sometimes caricatures. In their purest form, they are constructed round a single idea or quality; when there is more than one factor in them, we get the beginning of the curve towards the round. The really flat character can be expressed in one sentence such as 'I never will desert Mr Micawber'. There is Mrs Micawber – she says she won't desert Mr Micawber; she doesn't, and there she is. Or: 'I must conceal, even by subterfuges, the poverty of my master's house.' There is Caleb Balderstone in *The Bride of Lammermoor*. He does not use the actual phrase, but it completely describes him; he has no existence outside it, no pleasures, none of the private lusts and aches that must complicate the most consistent of servitors. Whatever he does, wherever he goes, whatever lies he tells or plates he breaks, it is to conceal the poverty of his master's house. It is not his *idée fixe*, because there is nothing in him into which the idea can be fixed. He *is* the idea, and such life as he possesses radiates from its edges and from the scintillations it strikes when other elements in the novel impinge. Or take Proust. There are numerous flat characters in Proust, such as the Princess of Parma, or Legrandin. Each can be expressed in a single sentence, the Princess's sentence being: 'I must be particularly careful to be kind.' She does nothing except to be particularly careful, and those of the other characters who are more complex than herself easily see through the kindness, since it is only a by-product of the carefulness.

One great advantage of flat characters is that they are easily recognized whenever they come in – recognized by the reader's emotional eye, not by the visual eye which merely notes the recurrence of a proper name. In Russian novels, where they so seldom occur, they would be a decided help. It is a convenience for an author when he can strike with his full force at once, and flat characters are very useful to him, since they never need reintroducing, never run away, have not to be watched for development, and provide their own atmosphere – little luminous discs of a pre-arranged size, pushed hither and thither like counters across the void or between the stars; most satisfactory.

A second advantage is that they are easily remembered by the reader afterwards. They remain in his mind as unalterable for the reason that they were not changed by circumstances; they moved through circumstances, which gives them in retrospect a comforting quality, and preserves them when the book that produced them may decay. The Countess in *Evan Harrington* furnishes a good little example here. Let us compare our memories of her with our memories of Becky Sharp. We do not remember what the Countess did or what she passed through. What is clear is her figure and the formula that surrounds it, namely, 'Proud as we are of dear papa, we must conceal his memory.' All her rich humour proceeds from this. She is a flat character. Becky is round. She, too, is on the make, but she cannot be summed up in a single phrase, and we remember her in connection with the great scenes through which she passed and as modified by those scenes – that is to say, we do not remember her so easily, because she waxes and wanes and has facets like a human being. All of us, even the sophisticated, yearn for permanence, and to the unsophisticated permanence is the chief excuse for a work of art. We all want books to endure, to be refuges, and their inhabitants to be always the same, and flat characters tend to justify themselves on this account.

All the same, critics who have their eyes fixed severely upon daily life – as were our eyes last week – have very little patience with such renderings of human nature. Queen Victoria, they argue, cannot be summed up in a single sentence, so what excuse remains for Mrs Micawber? One of our foremost writers, Mr Norman Douglas, is a critic of this type, and the passage from him which I will quote puts the case against flat characters in a forcible fashion. The passage occurs in an open letter to D. H. Lawrence, with whom he is quarrelling: a doughty pair of combatants, the hardness of whose hitting makes the rest of us feel like a lot of ladies up in a pavilion. He complains that Lawrence, in a biography of a mutual friend, has falsified the picture by employing 'the novelist's touch', and he goes on to define what this is:

It consists, I should say, in a failure to realize the profundities and complexities of the ordinary human mind; it selects for literary purposes two or three facets of a man or woman, generally the most spectacular and therefore 'useful' ingredients of their character, and disregards all the others. Whatever fails to fit in with these specially chosen traits is eliminated; must be eliminated, for otherwise the description would not hold water. Such and such are the data; everything incompatible with those data has to go by the board. It follows that the novelist's touch argues, often logically, from a wrong premise; it takes what it likes and leaves the rest. The facts may be correct so far as they go, but there are too few of them; what the author says may be true, and yet by no means the truth. That is the novelist's touch. It falsifies life.

Well, the novelist's touch as thus defined is, of course, bad in biography, for no human being is simple. But in a novel it has its place: a novel that is at all complex often requires flat people as well as round, and the outcome of their collisions parallels life more accurately than Mr Douglas implies. The case of Dickens is significant. Dickens's people are nearly all flat (Pip and David Copperfield attempt roundness, but so diffidently that they seem more like bubbles than solids). Nearly every one can be summed up in a sentence, and yet there is this wonderful feeling of human depth. Probably the immense vitality of Dickens causes his characters to vibrate a little, so that they borrow his life and appear to lead one of their own. It is a conjuring-trick; at any moment we may look at Mr Pickwick edgeways and find him no thicker than a gramophone record. But we never get the sideway view. Mr Pickwick is far too adroit and well-trained. He always has the air of weighing something, and when he is put into the cupboard of the young ladies' school he seems as heavy as Falstaff in the buck-basket at Windsor. Part of the genius of Dickens is that he does use types and caricatures, people whom we recognize the instant they re-enter, and yet achieves effects that are not mechanical and a vision of humanity that is not shallow. Those who dislike Dickens have an excellent case. He ought to be bad. He is actually one of our big writers, and his immense success with types suggests that there may be more in flatness than the severer critics admit.

Or take H. G. Wells. With the possible exceptions of Kipps and the aunt in *Tono-Bungay*, all Wells's characters are as flat as a photograph. But the photographs are agitated with such vigour that we forget their complexities lie on the surface and would disappear if it was scratched or curled up. A Wells character cannot indeed be summed up in a single phrase; he is tethered much more to observation, he does not create types. Nevertheless his people seldom pulsate by their own strength. It is the deft and powerful hands of their maker that shake them and trick the reader into a sense of depth. Good but imperfect novelists, like Wells and Dickens, are very clever at transmitting force. The part of their novel that is alive galvanizes the part that is not, and causes the characters to jump about and speak in a convincing way. They are quite different from the perfect novelist who touches all his material directly, who seems to pass the creative finger down every sentence and into every word. Richardson, Defoe, Jane Austen, are perfect in this particular way; their work may not be great but their hands are always upon it; there is not the tiny interval between the touching of the button and the sound of the bell which occurs in novels where the characters are not under direct control.

For we must admit that flat people are not in themselves as big achievements as round ones, and also that they are best when they are comic. A serious or tragic flat character is apt to be a bore. Each time he enters crying 'Revenge!' or 'My heart bleeds for humanity!' or whatever his formula is, our hearts sink. One of the romances of a popular contemporary writer is constructed round a Sussex farmer who says, 'I'll plough up that bit of gorse.' There is the farmer, there is the gorse; he says he'll plough it up, he does plough it up, but it is not like saying 'I never will desert Mr Micawber', because we are so bored by his consistency that we do not care whether he succeeds with the gorse or fails. If his formula was analysed and connected up with the rest of the human outfit, we should not be bored any longer, the formula would cease to be the man and become an obsession in the man; that is to say, he would have turned from a flat farmer into a round one. It is only round people who are fit to perform tragically for any length of time and can move us to any feelings except humour and appropriateness.

So now let us desert these two-dimensional people, and, by way of transition to the round, let us go to *Mansfield Park*, and look at Lady Bertram, sitting on her sofa with pug. Pug is flat, like most animals in fiction. He is once represented as straying into a rose-bed in a cardboard kind of way, but that is all, and during most of the book his mistress seems to be cut out of the same simple material as her dog. Lady Bertram's formula is 'I am kindly, but must not be fatigued', and she functions out of it. But at the end there is a catastrophe. Her two daughters come to grief – to the worst grief known to Miss Austen's universe, far worse than the Napoleonic wars. Julia elopes; Maria, who is unhappily married, runs off with a lover. What is Lady Bertram's reaction? The sentence describing it is significant:

> Lady Bertram did not think deeply, but, guided by Sir Thomas, she thought justly on all important points; and she saw, therefore, in all its enormity, what had happened, and neither endeavoured herself, nor required Fanny to advise her, to think little of guilt and infamy.

These are strong words, and they used to worry me because I thought Jane Austen's moral sense was getting out of hand. She may, and of course does, deprecate guilt and infamy herself, she duly causes distress in the minds of Edmund and Fanny, but has she any right to agitate calm, consistent Lady Bertram? Is not it like giving pug three faces and setting him to guard the gates of Hell? Ought not her ladyship to remain on the sofa saying, 'This is a dreadful and sadly exhausting business about Julia and Maria, but where is Fanny gone? I have dropped another stitch'?

I used to think this, through misunderstanding Jane Austen's method – exactly as Scott misunderstood it when he congratulated her for painting on a square of ivory. She is a miniaturist, but never two-dimensional. All her characters are round, or capable of rotundity. Even Miss Bates has a mind, even Elizabeth Elliot a heart, and Lady Bertram's moral fervour ceases to vex us when we realize this; the disc has suddenly extended and become a little globe. When the novel is closed, Lady Bertram goes back to the flat, it is true; the dominant impression she leaves can be summed up in a formula. But that is not how Jane Austen conceived her, and the freshness of her reappearances is due to this. Why do the characters in Jane Austen give us a slightly new pleasure each time they come in, as opposed to the merely repetitive pleasure that is caused by a character in Dickens? Why do they combine so well in a conversation, and draw one another out without seeming to do so, and never perform? The answer to this question can be put in several ways: that, unlike Dickens, she was a real artist, that she never stooped to caricature, etc. But the best reply is that her characters, though smaller than his, are more highly organized. They function all round, and even if her plot made greater demands on them than it does they would still be adequate. Suppose that Louisa Musgrove had broken her neck on the Cobb. The description of her death would have been feeble and ladylike – physical violence is quite beyond Miss Austen's powers – but the survivors would have reacted properly as soon as the corpse was carried away, they would have brought into view new sides of their character, and, though *Persuasion* would have been spoiled as a book, we should know more than we do about Captain Wentworth and Anne. All the Jane Austen characters are ready for an extended life, for a life which the scheme of her books seldom requires them to lead, and that is why they lead their actual lives so satisfactorily. Let us return to Lady Bertram and the crucial sentence. See how subtly it modulates from her formula into an area where the formula does not work. 'Lady Bertram did not think deeply.' Exactly: as per formula. 'But, guided by Sir Thomas, she thought justly on all important points.' Sir Thomas's guidance, which is part of the formula, remains, but it pushes her ladyship towards an independent and undesired morality. 'She saw, therefore, in all its enormity, what had happened.' This is the moral fortissimo – very strong but carefully introduced. And then follows a most artful decrescendo, by means of negatives. She 'neither endeavoured herself, nor required Fanny to advise her, to think little of guilt and infamy'. The formula is reappearing, because as a rule she does try to minimize trouble, and does require Fanny to advise her how to do this; indeed Fanny has done nothing else for the last ten years. The words, though they are negatived, remind us of this, her normal state is again in view, and she has in a single sentence been inflated into a round character and collapsed back into a flat one. How Jane Austen can write! In a few words she has extended Lady Bertram, and by so doing she has increased the probability of the elopements of Maria and Julia. I say probability because the elopements belong to the domain of violent physical action, and here, as already indicated, Jane Austen is feeble and ladylike. Except in her schoolgirl novels, she cannot stage a crash. Everything violent has to take place 'off' – Louisa's accident and Marianne Dashwood's putrid throat are the nearest exceptions – and consequently all the comments on the elopement must be sincere and convincing, otherwise we should doubt whether it occurred. Lady Bertram helps us to believe that her daughters have run away, and they have to run away, or there would be no apotheosis for Fanny. It is a little point, and a little sentence, yet it shows us how delicately a great novelist can modulate into the round.

All through her works we find these characters, apparently so simple and flat, never needing reintroduction and yet never out of their depth – Henry Tilney, Mr Woodhouse, Charlotte Lucas. She may label her characters 'Sense', 'Pride', 'Sensibility', 'Prejudice', but they are not tethered to those qualities.

As for the round characters proper, they have already been defined by implication and no more need be said. All I need do is to give some examples of people in books who seem to me round, so that the definition can be tested afterwards:

All the principal characters in *War and Peace*, all the Dostoyevsky characters, and some of the Proust – for example, the old family servant, the Duchess of Guermantes, M. de

Charlus, and Saint-Loup; Madame Bovary – who, like Moll Flanders, has her book to herself, and can expand and secrete unchecked; some people in Thackeray – for instance, Becky and Beatrix; some in Fielding – Parson Adams, Tom Jones; and some in Charlotte Brontë, most particularly Lucy Snowe. (And many more – this is not a catalogue.) The test of a round character is whether it is capable of surprising in a convincing way. If it never surprises, it is flat. If it does not convince, it is flat pretending to be round. It has the incalculability of life about it – life within the pages of a book. And by using it sometimes alone, more often in combination with the other kind, the novelist achieves his task of acclimatization, and harmonizes the human race with the other aspects of his work.

2

Now for the second device: the point of view from which the story may be told.

To some critics this is the fundamental device.

The whole intricate question of method, in the craft of fiction [says Mr Percy Lubbock], I take to be governed by the question of the point of view – the question of the relation in which the narrator stands to the story.

And his book *The Craft of Fiction* examines various points of view with genius and insight. The novelist, he says, can either describe the characters from outside, as an impartial or partial onlooker; or he can assume omniscience and describe them from within; or he can place himself in the position of one of them and affect to be in the dark as to the motives of the rest; or there are certain intermediate attitudes.

Those who follow him will lay a sure foundation for the aesthetics of fiction – a foundation which I cannot for a moment promise. This is a ramshackly survey, and for me the whole intricate question of method resolves itself not into formulae but into the power of the writer to bounce the reader into accepting what he says – a power which Mr Lubbock admits and admires, but locates at the edge of the problem instead of at the centre. I should put it plumb in the centre. Look how Dickens bounces us in *Bleak House*. Chapter 1 of *Bleak House* is omniscient. Dickens takes us into the Court of Chancery and rapidly explains all the people there. In Chapter 2 he is partially omniscient. We still use his eyes, but for some unexplained reason they begin to grow weak: he can explain Sir Leicester Dedlock to us, part of Lady Dedlock but not all, and nothing of Mr Tulkinghorn. In Chapter 3 he is even more reprehensible: he goes straight across into the dramatic method and inhabits a young lady, Esther Summerson. 'I have a great deal of difficulty in beginning to write my portion of these pages, for I know I am not clever,' pipes up Esther, and continues in this strain with consistency and competence, so long as she is allowed to hold the pen. At any moment the author of her being may snatch it from her, and run about taking notes himself, leaving her seated goodness knows where, and employed we do not care how. Logically, *Bleak House* is all to pieces, but Dickens bounces us, so that we do not mind the shiftings of the viewpoint.

Critics are more apt to object than readers. Zealous for the novel's eminence, they are a little too apt to look out for problems that shall be peculiar to it, and differentiate it from the drama; they feel it ought to have its own technical troubles before it can be accepted as an independent art; and since the problem of a point of view certainly is peculiar to the novel they have rather overstressed it. I do not myself think it is so important as a proper mixture of characters – a problem which the dramatist is up against also. And the novelist must bounce us; that is imperative.

Let us glance at two other examples of a shifting viewpoint.

The eminent French writer André Gide has published a

novel called *Les Faux-Monnayeurs*[1] of which there will be more
to say next week: a novel which for all its modernity has one
aspect in common with *Bleak House*: it is all to pieces logically.
Sometimes the author is omniscient: he explains everything,
he stands back, 'il juge ses personnages'; at other times his
omniscience is partial; yet again he is dramatic, and causes
the story to be told through the diary of one of the characters.
There is the same absence of viewpoint, but, whereas in
Dickens it was instinctive, in Gide it is sophisticated; he ex-
patiates too much about the jolts. The novelist who betrays
too much interest in his own method can never be more than
interesting; he has given up the creation of character and
summoned us to help analyse his own mind, and a heavy drop
in the emotional thermometer results. *Les Faux-Monnayeurs* is
among the more interesting of recent works; not among the
vital; and greatly as we shall have to admire it as a fabric we
cannot praise it unrestrictedly now.

For our second example we must again glance at *War and
Peace*. Here the result is vital: we are bounced up and down
Russia – omniscient, semi-omniscient, dramatized here or
there as the moment dictates – and at the end we have accepted it all. Mr Lubbock does not, it is true: great as he finds
the book, he would find it greater if it had a viewpoint; he
feels Tolstoy has not pulled his full weight. I feel that the rules
of the game of writing are not like this. A novelist can shift his
viewpoint if it comes off, and it came off with Dickens and
Tolstoy. Indeed this power to expand and contract perception (of which the shifting viewpoint is a symptom), this right
to intermittent knowledge – I find it one of the great advantages of the novel-form, and it has a parallel in our perception
of life. We are stupider at some times than others; we can
enter into people's minds occasionally but not always, because our own minds get tired; and this intermittence lends in

1. Translated by Dorothy Bussy as *The Counterfeiters* (Knopf). [In print
under this title as a Penguin Modern Classic.]

the long run variety and colour to the experiences we receive. A quantity of novelists, English novelists especially, have behaved like this to the people in their books: played fast and loose with them, and I cannot see why they should be censured.

They must be censured if we catch them at it at the time. That is quite true, and out of it arises another question: may the writer take the reader into his confidence about his characters? Answer has already been indicated: better not. It is dangerous, it generally leads to a drop in the temperature, to intellectual and emotional laxity, and worse still to facetiousness, and to a friendly invitation to see how the figures hook up behind. 'Doesn't A look nice – she always was my favourite.' 'Let's think of why B does that – perhaps there's more in him than meets the eye – yes, see – he has a heart of gold – having given you this peep at it I'll pop it back – I don't think he's noticed.' 'And C – he always was the mystery man.' Intimacy is gained but at the expense of illusion and nobility. It is like standing a man a drink so that he may not criticize your opinions. With all respect to Fielding and Thackeray, it is devastating, it is bar-parlour chattiness, and nothing has been more harmful to the novels of the past. To take your reader into your confidence about the universe is a different thing. It is not dangerous for a novelist to draw back from his characters, as Hardy and Conrad do, and to generalize about the conditions under which he thinks life is carried on. It is confidences about the individual people that do harm, and beckon the reader away from the people to an examination of the novelist's mind. Not much is ever found in it at such a moment, for it is never in the creative state: the mere process of saying 'Come along, let's have a chat' has cooled it down.

Our comments on human beings must now come to an end. They may take fuller shape when we come to discuss the plot.

5

THE PLOT

'CHARACTER,' says Aristotle, 'gives us qualities, but it is in actions – what we do – that we are happy or the reverse.' We have already decided that Aristotle is wrong, and now we must face the consequences of disagreeing with him. 'All human happiness and misery,' says Aristotle, 'take the form of action.' We know better. We believe that happiness and misery exist in the secret life, which each of us leads privately and to which (in his characters) the novelist has access. And by the secret life we mean the life for which there is no external evidence, not, as is vulgarly supposed, that which is revealed by a chance word or a sigh. A chance word or sigh are just as much evidence as a speech or a murder: the life they reveal ceases to be secret and enters the realm of action.

There is, however, no occasion to be hard on Aristotle. He had read few novels and no modern ones – the *Odyssey* but not *Ulysses* – he was by temperament apathetic to secrecy, and indeed regarded the human mind as a sort of tub from which everything can finally be extracted; and when he wrote the words quoted above he had in view the drama, where no doubt they hold true. In the drama all human happiness and misery does and must take the form of action. Otherwise its existence remains unknown, and this is the great difference between the drama and the novel.

The speciality of the novel is that the writer can talk about his characters as well as through them, or can arrange for us to listen when they talk to themselves. He has access to self-communings, and from that level he can descend even deeper and peer into the subconscious. A man does not talk to himself quite truly – not even to himself; the happiness or misery that

85

he secretly feels proceed from causes that he cannot quite explain, because as soon as he raises them to the level of the explicable they lose their native quality. The novelist has a real pull here. He can show the subconscious short-circuiting straight into action (the dramatist can do this too); he can also show it in its relation to soliloquy. He commands all the secret life, and he must not be robbed of this privilege. 'How did the writer know that?' it is sometimes said. 'What's his standpoint? He is not being consistent, he's shifting his point of view from the limited to the omniscient, and now he's edging back again.' Questions like these have too much the atmosphere of the law courts about them. All that matters to the reader is whether the shifting of attitude and the secret life are convincing, whether it is πιθανόν in fact, and with his favourite word ringing in his ears Aristotle may retire.

However, he leaves us in some confusion, for what, with this enlargement of human nature, is going to become of the plot? In most literary works there are two elements: human individuals, whom we have recently discussed, and the element vaguely called art. Art we have also dallied with, but with a very low form of it, the story: the chopped-off length of the tapeworm of time. Now we arrive at a much higher aspect, the plot; and the plot, instead of finding human beings more or less cut to its requirements, as they are in the drama, finds them enormous, shadowy and intractable, and three-quarters hidden like an iceberg. In vain it points out to these unwieldy creatures the advantages of the triple process of complication, crisis and solution so persuasively expounded by Aristotle. A few of them rise and comply, and a novel which ought to have been a play is the result. But there is no general response. They want to sit apart and brood or something, and the plot (whom I here visualize as a sort of higher government official) is concerned at their lack of public spirit: 'This will not do,' it seems to say. 'Individualism is a most valuable quality; indeed my own position depends upon individuals;

I have always admitted as much freely. Nevertheless there are certain limits, and those limits are being overstepped. Characters must not brood too long, they must not waste time running up and down ladders in their own insides, they must contribute, or higher interests will be jeopardized.' How well one knows that phrase, 'a contribution to the plot'! It is accorded, and of necessity, by the people in a drama; how necessary is it in a novel?

Let us define a plot. We have defined a story as a narrative of events arranged in their time-sequence. A plot is also a narrative of events, the emphasis falling on causality. 'The king died and then the queen died' is a story. 'The king died, and then the queen died of grief' is a plot. The time-sequence is preserved, but the sense of causality overshadows it. Or again: 'The queen died, no one knew why, until it was discovered that it was through grief at the death of the king.' This is a plot with a mystery in it, a form capable of high development. It suspends the time-sequence, it moves as far away from the story as its limitations will allow. Consider the death of the queen. If it is in a story we say: 'And then?' If it is in a plot we ask: 'Why?' That is the fundamental difference between these two aspects of the novel. A plot cannot be told to a gaping audience of cave-men or to a tyrannical sultan or to their modern descendant the movie-public. They can only be kept awake by 'And then – and then –' they can only supply curiosity. But a plot demands intelligence and memory also.

Curiosity is one of the lowest of the human faculties. You will have noticed in daily life that when people are inquisitive they nearly always have bad memories and are usually stupid at bottom. The man who begins by asking you how many brothers and sisters you have is never a sympathetic character, and if you meet him in a year's time he will probably ask you how many brothers and sisters you have, his mouth again sagging open, his eyes still bulging from his head. It is difficult to be friends with such a man, and for two inquisitive people to be friends must be impossible. Curiosity by itself takes us a very little way, nor does it take us far into the novel – only as far as the story. If we would grasp the plot we must add intelligence and memory.

Intelligence first. The intelligent novel-reader, unlike the inquisitive one who just runs his eye over a new fact, mentally picks it up. He sees it from two points of view: isolated, and related to the other facts that he has read on previous pages. Probably he does not understand it, but he does not expect to do so yet awhile. The facts in a highly organized novel (like *The Egoist*) are often of the nature of cross-correspondences, and the ideal spectator cannot expect to view them properly until he is sitting up on a hill at the end. This element of surprise or mystery – the detective element as it is sometimes rather emptily called – is of great importance in a plot. It occurs through a suspension of the time-sequence; a mystery is a pocket in time, and it occurs crudely, as in 'Why did the queen die?', and more subtly in half-explained gestures and words, the true meaning of which only dawns pages ahead. Mystery is essential to a plot, and cannot be appreciated without intelligence. To the curious it is just another 'And then –' To appreciate a mystery, part of the mind must be left behind, brooding, while the other part goes marching on.

That brings us to our second qualification: memory.

Memory and intelligence are closely connected, for unless we remember we cannot understand. If by the time the queen dies we have forgotten the existence of the king we shall never make out what killed her. The plot-maker expects us to remember, we expect him to leave no loose ends. Every action or word in a plot ought to count; it ought to be economical and spare; even when complicated it should be organic and free from dead matter. It may be difficult or easy, it may and should contain mysteries, but it ought not to mislead. And over it, as it unfolds, will hover the memory of the reader (that dull glow of the mind of which intelligence is the bright advancing edge) and will constantly rearrange and reconsider, seeing new clues, new chains of cause and effect, and the final sense (if the plot has been a fine one) will not be of clues or chains, but of something aesthetically compact, something which might have been shown by the novelist straight away, only if he had shown it straight away it would never have become beautiful. We come up against beauty here – for the first time in our enquiry: beauty at which a novelist should never aim, though he fails if he does not achieve it. I will conduct beauty to her proper place later on. Meanwhile please accept her as part of a completed plot. She looks a little surprised at being there, but beauty ought to look a little surprised; it is the emotion that best suits her face, as Botticelli knew when he painted her risen from the waves, between the winds and the flowers. The beauty who does not look surprised, who accepts her position as her due – she reminds us too much of a prima donna.

But let us get back to the plot, and we will do so via George Meredith.

Meredith is not the great name he was twenty or thirty years ago, when much of the universe and all Cambridge trembled. I remember how depressed I used to be by a line in one of his poems: 'We breathe but to be sword or block.' I did not want to be either and I knew that I was not a sword. It seems, though, that there was no real cause for depression, for Meredith is himself now rather in the trough of a wave, and though fashion will turn and raise him a bit he will never be the spiritual power he was about the year 1900. His philosophy has not worn well. His heavy attacks on sentimentality – they bore the present generation, which pursues the same quarry but with neater instruments, and is apt to suspect anyone carrying a blunderbuss of being a sentimentalist himself. And his visions of Nature – they do not endure like Hardy's, there is too much Surrey about them, they are fluffy and lush.

He could no more write the opening chapter of *The Return of the Native* than Box Hill could visit Salisbury Plain. What is really tragic and enduring in the scenery of England was hidden from him, and so is what is really tragic in life. When he gets serious and noble-minded there is a strident overtone, a bullying that becomes distressing. I feel indeed that he was like Tennyson in one respect: through not taking himself quietly enough he strained his inside. And his novels: most of the social values are faked. The tailors are not tailors, the cricket matches are not cricket, the railway trains do not even seem to be trains, the county families give the air of having been only just that moment unpacked, scarcely in position before the action starts, the straw still clinging to their beards. It is surely very odd, the social scene in which his characters are set; it is partly due to his fantasy, which is legitimate, but partly a chilly fake, and wrong. What with the faking, what with the preaching, which was never agreeable and is now said to be hollow, and what with the home counties posing as the universe, it is no wonder Meredith now lies in the trough. And yet he is in one way a great novelist. He is the finest contriver that English fiction has ever produced, and any lecture on plot must do homage to him.

Meredith's plots are not closely knit. We cannot describe the action of *Harry Richmond* in a phrase, as we can *Great Expectations*', though both books turn on the mistake made by a young man as to the sources of his fortune. A Meredithian plot is not a temple to the tragic or even to the comic Muse, but rather resembles a series of kiosks most artfully placed among wooded slopes, which his people reach by their own impetus, and from which they emerge with altered aspect. Incident springs out of character, and having occurred it alters that character. People and events are closely connected, and he does it by means of these contrivances. They are often delightful, sometimes touching, always unexpected. This shock, followed by the feeling 'Oh, that's all right', is a sign that all is well with the plot; characters, to be real, ought to run smoothly, but a plot ought to cause surprise. The horse-whipping of Dr Shrapnel in *Beauchamp's Career* is a surprise. We know that Everard Romfrey must dislike Shrapnel, must hate and misunderstand his radicalism, and be jealous of his influence over Beauchamp; we watch too the growth of the misunderstanding over Rosamund, we watch the intrigues of Cecil Baskelett. As far as characters go, Meredith plays with his cards on the table, but when the incident comes what a shock it gives us and the characters too! The tragi-comic business of one old man whipping another from the highest motives – it reacts upon all their world, and transforms all the personages of the book. It is not the centre of *Beauchamp's Career*, which indeed has no centre. It is essentially a contrivance, a door through which the book is made to pass, emerging in an altered form. Towards the close, when Beauchamp is drowned and Shrapnel and Romfrey are reconciled over his body, there is an attempt to elevate the plot to Aristotelean symmetry, to turn the novel into a temple wherein dwells interpretation and peace. Meredith fails here: *Beauchamp's Career* remains a series of contrivances (the visit to France is another of them), but contrivances that spring from the characters and react upon them.

And now briefly to illustrate the mystery element in the plot: the formula of 'the queen died, it was afterwards discovered, through grief'. I will take an example, not from Dickens (though *Great Expectations* provides a fine one), nor from Conan Doyle (whom my priggishness prevents me from enjoying), but again from Meredith: an example of a concealed emotion from the admirable plot of *The Egoist*: it occurs in the character of Laetitia Dale.

We are told, at first, all that passes in Laetitia's mind. Sir Willoughby has twice jilted her, she is sad, resigned. Then, for dramatic reasons, her mind is hidden from us, it develops naturally enough, but does not re-emerge until the great midnight scene where he asks her to marry him because he is not sure about Clara, and this time, a changed woman, Laetitia says 'No'. Meredith has concealed the change. It would have spoiled his high comedy if we had been kept in touch with it throughout. Sir Willoughby has to have a series of crashes, to catch at this and that, and find everything rickety. We should not enjoy the fun, in fact it would be boorish, if we saw the author preparing the booby-traps beforehand, so Laetitia's apathy has been hidden from us. This is one of the countless examples in which either plot or character has to suffer, and Meredith with his unerring good sense here lets the plot triumph.

As an example of mistaken triumph, I think of a slip – it is no more than a slip – which Charlotte Brontë makes in *Villette*. She allows Lucy Snowe to conceal from the reader her discovery that Dr John is the same as her old playmate Graham. When it comes out, we do get a good plot-thrill, but too much at the expense of Lucy's character. She has seemed, up to then, the spirit of integrity, and has, as it were, laid herself under a moral obligation to narrate all that she knows. That she stoops to suppress is a little distressing, though the incident is too trivial to do her any permanent harm.

Sometimes a plot triumphs too completely. The characters have to suspend their natures at every turn, or else are so swept away by the course of fate that our sense of their reality is weakened. We shall find instances of this in a writer who is far greater than Meredith, and yet less successful as a novelist – Thomas Hardy. Hardy seems to me essentially a poet, who conceives of his novels from an enormous height. They are to be tragedies or tragi-comedies, they are to give out the sound of hammer-strokes as they proceed; in other words Hardy arranges events with emphasis on causality, the ground-plan is a plot, and the characters are ordered to acquiesce in its requirements. Except in the person of Tess (who conveys the feeling that she is greater than destiny), this aspect of his work is unsatisfactory. His characters are involved in various snares, they are finally bound hand and foot, there is ceaseless emphasis on fate, and yet, for all the sacrifices made to it, we never see the action as a living thing as we see it in *Antigone* or *Bérénice* or *The Cherry Orchard*. The fate above us, not the fate working through us – that is what is eminent and memorable in the Wessex novels. Egdon Heath before Eustacia Vye has set foot upon it. The woods without the Woodlanders. The downs above Budmouth Regis with royal princesses, still asleep, driving across them through the dawn. Hardy's success in *The Dynasts* (where he uses another medium) is complete, there the hammer-strokes are heard, cause and effect enchain the characters despite their struggles, complete contact between the actors and the plot is established. But in the novels, though the same superb and terrible machine works, it never catches humanity in its teeth; there is some vital problem that has not been answered, or even posed, in the misfortunes of Jude the Obscure. In other words the characters have been required to contribute too much to the plot; except in their rustic humours, their vitality has been impoverished, they have gone dry and thin. This, as far as I can make out, is the flaw running through Hardy's novels: he has emphasized causality more strongly than his medium permits. As a poet and prophet and visualizer George Meredith is nothing by his side – just a suburban roarer – but Meredith did know what the novel could stand, where the plot could dun the characters for a contribution, where it must let them function as they liked. And the moral – well, I see no moral, because the work of Hardy is my home and that of Meredith cannot be; still, the moral from the point of these lectures is again unfavourable to Aristotle. In the novel, all human happiness and misery does not take the form of action, it seeks means of expression other than through the plot, it must not be rigidly canalized.

In the losing battle that the plot fights with the characters, it often takes a cowardly revenge. Nearly all novels are feeble at the end. This is because the plot requires to be wound up. Why is this necessary? Why is there not a convention which allows a novelist to stop as soon as he feels bored? Alas, he has to round things off, and usually the characters go dead while he is at work, and our final impression of them is through deadness. *The Vicar of Wakefield* is in this way a typical novel, so clever and fresh in the first half, up to the painting of the family group with Mrs Primrose as Venus, and then so wooden and imbecile. Incidents and people that occurred at first for their own sake now have to contribute to the dénouement. In the end even the author feels he is being a little foolish. 'Nor can I go on,' he says, 'without a reflection on those accidental meetings which, though they happen every day, seldom excite our surprise but upon some extraordinary occasion.' Goldsmith is of course a lightweight, but most novels do fail here – there is this disastrous standstill while logic takes over the command from flesh and blood. If it was not for death and marriage I do not know how the average novelist would conclude. Death and marriage are almost his only connection between his characters and his plot, and the reader is more ready to meet him here, and take a bookish view of them, provided they occur later on in the book; the writer, poor fellow, must be allowed to finish up somehow, he has his living to get like anyone else, so no wonder that nothing is heard but hammering and screwing.

This, as far as one can generalize, is the inherent defect of novels: they go off at the end; and there are two explanations: firstly, failure of pep, which threatens the novelist like all workers; and, secondly, the difficulty which we have been discussing. The characters have been getting out of hand, laying foundations and declining to build on them afterwards, and now the novelist has to labour personally, in order that the job may be done to time. He pretends that the characters are acting for him. He keeps mentioning their names and using inverted commas. But the characters are gone or dead.

The plot, then, is the novel in its logical intellectual aspect; it requires mystery, but the mysteries are solved later on; the reader may be moving about in worlds unrealized, but the novelist has no misgivings. He is competent, poised above his work, throwing a beam of light here, popping on a cap of invisibility there, and (qua plot-maker) continually negotiating with himself qua character-monger as to the best effect to be produced. He plans his book beforehand; or anyhow he stands above it, his interest in cause and effect gives him an air of predetermination.

And now we must ask ourselves whether the framework thus produced is the best possible for a novel. After all, why has a novel to be planned? Cannot it grow? Why need it close, as a play closes? Cannot it open out? Instead of standing above his work and controlling it, cannot the novelist throw himself into it and be carried along to some goal that he does not foresee? The plot is exciting and may be beautiful, yet is it not a fetish, borrowed from the drama, from the spatial limitations of the stage? Cannot fiction devise a framework that is not so logical yet more suitable to its genius?

Modern writers say that it can, and we will now examine a recent example: a violent onslaught on the plot as we have defined it, and a constructive attempt to put something in the place of the plot.

I have already mentioned the novel in question: *Les Faux-Monnayeurs* by André Gide. It contains within its covers both the methods. Gide has also published the diary he kept while he was writing the novel, and there is no reason why he should not publish in the future the impressions he had when re-reading both the diary and the novel, and in the future perfect a still more final synthesis in which the diary, the novel and his impressions of both will interact. He is indeed a little more solemn than an author should be about the whole caboodle, but regarded as a caboodle it is excessively interesting, and repays careful study by critics.

We have, in the first place, a plot in *Les Faux-Monnayeurs* of the logical objective type that we have been considering – a plot, or rather fragments of plots. The main fragment concerns a young man called Olivier – a charming, touching and lovable character, who misses happiness, and then recovers it after an excellently contrived dénouement; confers it also; this fragment has a wonderful radiance and 'lives', if I may use so coarse a word, it is a successful creation on familiar lines. But it is by no means the centre of the book. No more are the other logical fragments – that which concerns Georges, Olivier's schoolboy brother, who passes false coin, and is instrumental in driving a fellow pupil to suicide. (Gide gives us his sources for all this in his diary: he got the idea of Georges from a boy whom he caught trying to steal a book off a stall, the gang of coiners were caught at Rouen, and the suicide of children took place at Clermont-Ferrand, etc.) Neither Olivier, nor Georges, nor Vincent a third brother, nor Bernard their friend is the centre of the book. We come nearer to it in Edouard. Edouard is a novelist. He bears the same relation to Gide as Clissold does to Wells. I dare not be more precise. Like Gide, he keeps a diary, like Gide he is writing a book called *Les Faux-Monnayeurs*, and like Clissold he is disavowed. Edouard's diary is printed in full. It begins before the plot-fragments, continues during them, and forms the bulk of Gide's book. Edouard is not just a chronicler. He is an actor too; indeed it is he who rescues Olivier and is rescued by him; we leave those two in happiness.

But that is still not the centre. The nearest to the centre lies in a discussion about the art of the novel. Edouard is holding forth to Bernard his secretary and some friends. He has said that truth in life and truth in a novel are not identical, and that he wants to write a book which shall include both sorts of truth.

'And what is its subject?' asked Sophroniska.

'There is none,' said Edouard sharply. 'My novel has no

subject. No doubt that sounds foolish. Let us say, if you prefer, that it will not have "a" subject . . . "A slice of life," the naturalistic school used to say. The mistake that school made was always to cut its slice in the same direction, always lengthwise, in the direction of time. Why not cut it up and down? Or across? As for me, I don't want to cut it at all. You see what I mean. I want to put everything into my novel and not snip off my material either here or there. I have been working for a year, and there is nothing I haven't put in: all I see, all I know, all I can learn from other people's lives and my own.'

'My poor man, you will bore your readers to death,' cried Laura, unable to restrain her mirth.

'Not at all. To get my effect, I am inventing, as my central character, a novelist, and the subject of my book will be the struggle between what reality offers him and what he tries to make of the offer.'

'Have you planned out this book?' asked Sophroniska, trying to keep grave.

'Of course not.'

'Why "of course"?'

'For a book of this type any plan would be unsuitable. The whole of it would go wrong if I decided any detail ahead. I am waiting for reality to dictate to me.'

'But I thought you wanted to get away from reality.'

'My novelist wants to get away, but I keep pulling him back. To tell the truth, this is my subject: the struggle between facts as proposed by reality, and the ideal reality.'

'Do tell us the name of this book,' said Laura, in despair.

'Very well. Tell it them, Bernard.'

'*Les Faux-Monnayeurs*,' said Bernard. 'And now will you please tell us who these *faux-monnayeurs* are.'

'I haven't the least idea.'

Bernard and Laura looked at each other and then at Sophroniska. There was the sound of a deep sigh.

The fact was that ideas about money, depreciation, inflation, forgery, etc., had gradually invaded Edouard's book – just as theories of clothing invade *Sartor Resartus* and even assume the functions of characters. 'Has anyone here ever had hold of a false coin?' he asked after a pause. 'Imagine a ten-franc piece, gold, false. It is actually worth a couple of sous, but it will remain worth ten francs until it is found out. Suppose I begin with the idea that –'

'But why begin with an idea?' burst out Bernard, who was by now in a state of exasperation. 'Why not begin with a fact? If you introduce the fact properly, the idea will follow of itself. If I was writing your *Faux-Monnayeurs* I should begin with a piece of false money, with the ten-franc piece you were speaking of, and here it is!'

So saying, Bernard pulled a ten-franc piece out of his pocket and flung it on the table.

'There,' he remarked. 'It rings all right. I got it this morning from the grocer. It's worth more than a couple of sous, as it's coated in gold, but it's actually made of glass. It will become quite transparent in time. No – don't rub it – you're going to spoil my false coin.'

Edouard had taken it and was examining it with the utmost attention.

'How did the grocer get it?'

'He doesn't know. He passed it on me for a joke, and then enlightened me, being a decent fellow. He let me have it for five francs. I thought that, since you were writing *Les Faux-Monnayeurs*, you ought to see what false money is like, so I got it to show you. Now that you have looked at it, give it me back. I am sorry to see that reality has no interest for you.'

'Yes,' said Edouard; 'it interests me, but it puts me out.'

'That's a pity,' remarked Bernard.[1]

This passage is the centre of the book. It contains the old thesis of truth in life versus truth in art, and illustrates it very neatly by the arrival of an actual false coin. What is new in it is the attempt to combine the two truths, the proposal that writers should mix themselves up in their material and be rolled over and over by it; they should not try to subdue any

1. Paraphrased from *Les Faux-Monnayeurs*, pp. 238–46. My version, needless to say, conveys neither the subtlety nor the balance of the original.

longer, they should hope to be subdued, to be carried away. As for a plot – to pot with the plot! Break it up, boil it down. Let there be those 'formidable erosions of contour' of which Nietzsche speaks. All that is prearranged is false.

Another distinguished critic has agreed with Gide – that old lady in the anecdote who was accused by her nieces of being illogical. For some time she could not be brought to understand what logic was, and when she grasped its true nature she was not so much angry as contemptuous. 'Logic! Good gracious! What rubbish!' she exclaimed. 'How can I tell what I think till I see what I say?' Her nieces, educated young women, thought that she was *passée*; she was really more up-to-date than they were.

Those who are in touch with contemporary France say that the present generation follows the advice of Gide and the old lady, and resolutely hurls itself into confusion, and indeed admires English novelists on the ground that they so seldom succeed in what they attempt. Compliments are always delightful, but this particular one is a bit of a backhander. It is like trying to lay an egg and being told you have produced a paraboloid – more curious than gratifying. And what results when you try to lay a paraboloid, I cannot conceive – perhaps the death of the hen. That seems the danger in Gide's position – he sets out to lay a paraboloid; he is not well advised, if he wants to write subconscious novels, to reason so lucidly and patiently about the subconscious; he is introducing mysticism at the wrong stage of the process. However, that is his affair. As a critic he is most stimulating, and the various bundles of words he has called *Les Faux-Monnayeurs* will be enjoyed by all who cannot tell what they think till they see what they say, or who weary of tyranny by the plot and of its alternative, tyranny by characters.

There is clearly something else in view, some other aspect or aspects which we have yet to examine. We may suspect the claim to be consciously subconscious, nevertheless there is a vague and vast residue into which the subconscious enters. Poetry, religion, passion – we have not placed them yet, and since we are critics – only critics – we must try to place them, to catalogue the rainbow. We have already peeped and botanized upon our mothers' graves.

The numbering of the warp and woof of the rainbow must accordingly be attempted, and we must now bring our minds to bear on the subject of fantasy.

6

FANTASY

A COURSE of lectures, if it is to be more than a collection of remarks, must have an idea running through it. It must also have a subject, and the idea ought to run through the subject too. This is so obvious as to sound foolish, but anyone who has tried to lecture will realize that here is a genuine difficulty. A course, like any other collection of words, generates an atmosphere. It has its own apparatus – a lecturer, an audience or provision for one – it occurs at regular intervals, it is announced by printed notices, and it has a financial side, though this last is tactfully concealed. Thus it tends in its parasitic way to lead a life of its own, and it and the idea running through it are apt to move in one direction while the subject steals off in the other.

The idea running through these lectures is by now plain enough: that there are in the novel two forces: human beings and a bundle of various things not human beings, and that it is the novelist's business to adjust these two forces and conciliate their claims. That is plain enough, but does it run through the novel too? Perhaps our subject, namely the books we have read, has stolen away from us while we theorize, like a shadow from an ascending bird. The bird is all right – it climbs, it is consistent and eminent. The shadow is all right – it has flickered across roads and gardens. But the two things resemble one another less and less, they do not touch as they did when the bird rested its toes on the ground. Criticism, especially a critical course, is so misleading. However lofty its intentions and sound its method, its subject slides away from beneath it, imperceptibly away, and lecturer and audience may awake with a start to find that they are carrying on in a distinguished and intelligent manner, but in regions which have nothing to do with anything they have read.

It was this that was worrying Gide, or rather one of the things that was worrying him, for he has an anxious mind. When we try to translate truth out of one sphere into another, whether from life into books or from books into lectures, something happens to truth: it goes wrong, not suddenly, when it might be detected, but slowly. That long passage from *Les Faux-Monnayeurs* already quoted may recall the bird to its shadow. It is not possible, after it, to apply the old apparatus any more. There is more in the novel than time or people or logic or any of their derivatives, more even than fate. And by 'more' I do not mean something that excludes these aspects nor something that includes them, embraces them. I mean something that cuts across them like a bar of light, that is intimately connected with them at one place and patiently illumines all their problems, and at another place shoots over or through them as if they did not exist. We shall give that bar of light two names, fantasy and prophecy.

The novels we have now to consider all tell a story, contain characters, and have plots or bits of plots, so we could apply to them the apparatus suited for Fielding or Arnold Bennett. But when I say two of their names – *Tristram Shandy* and *Moby Dick* – it is clear that we must stop and think a moment. The bird and the shadow are too far apart. A new formula must be found; the mere fact that one can mention Tristram and Moby in a single sentence shows it. What an impossible pair! As far apart as the poles. Yes. And like the poles they have one thing in common, which the lands round the equator do not share: an axis. What is essential in Sterne and Melville belongs to this new aspect of fiction: the fantastic-prophetical axis. George Meredith touched it: he was somewhat fantastic. So did Charlotte

Brontë: she was a prophetess occasionally. But in neither of these was it essential. Deprive them of it, and a book remains which still resembles *Harry Richmond* or *Shirley*. Deprive Sterne or Melville of it, deprive Peacock or Max Beerbohm or Virginia Woolf or Walter de la Mare or William Beckford or James Joyce or D. H. Lawrence or Swift, and nothing is left at all.

Our easiest approach to a definition of any aspect of fiction is always by considering the sort of demand it makes on the reader. Curiosity for the story, human feelings and a sense of value for the characters, intelligence and memory for the plot. What does fantasy ask of us? It asks us to pay something extra. It compels us to an adjustment that is different to an adjustment required by a work of art, to an additional adjustment. The other novelists say, 'Here is something that might occur in your lives,' the fantasist: 'Here is something that could not occur. I must ask you first to accept my book as a whole, and secondly to accept certain things in my book.' Many readers can grant the first request, but refuse the second. 'One knows a book isn't real,' they say; 'still, one does expect it to be natural, and this angel or midget or ghost or silly delay about the child's birth – no, it is too much.' They either retract their original concession and stop reading, or if they do go on it is with complete coldness, and they watch the gambols of the author without realizing how much they may mean to him.

No doubt the above approach is not critically sound. We all know that a work of art is an entity, etc. etc.; it has its own laws which are not those of daily life, anything that suits it is true, so why should any question arise about the angel, etc., except whether it is suitable to its book? Why place an angel on a different basis from a stockbroker? Once in the realm of the fictitious, what difference is there between an apparition and a mortgage? I see the soundness of this argument, but my heart refuses to assent. The general tone of novels is so literal that when the fantastic is introduced it produces a special effect; some readers are thrilled, others choked off; it demands an additional adjustment because of the oddness of its method or subject-matter – like a side-show in an exhibition where you pay sixpence as well as the original entrance fee. Some readers pay with delight, it is only for the side-shows that they entered the exhibition, and it is only to them I can address myself now. Others refuse with indignation, and these have our sincere regards, for to dislike the fantastic in literature is not to dislike literature. It does not even imply poverty of imagination, only a disinclination to meet certain demands that are made on it. Mr Asquith (if gossip is correct) could not meet the demands made on him by *Lady into Fox*. He should not have objected, he said, if the fox had become a lady again, but as it was he was left with an uncomfortable dissatisfied feeling. This feeling reflects no discredit either upon an eminent politician or a charming book. It merely means that Mr Asquith, though a genuine lover of literature, could not pay the additional sixpence – or rather he was willing to pay it but hoped to get it back again at the end.

So fantasy asks us to pay something extra.

Let us now distinguish between fantasy and prophecy.

They are alike in having gods, and unlike in the gods they have. There is in both the sense of mythology which differentiates them from other aspects of our subject. An invocation is again possible, therefore on behalf of fantasy let us now invoke all beings who inhabit the lower air, the shallow water and the smaller hills, all Fauns and Dryads and slips of the memory, all verbal coincidences, Pans and puns, all that is medieval this side of the grave. When we come to prophecy we shall utter no invocation, but it will have been to whatever transcends our abilities even when it is human passion that transcends them, to the deities of **India, Greece, Scandinavia and Judaea, to all that is** medieval beyond the grave and to Lucifer son of the morning. By their mythologies we shall distinguish these two sorts of novels.

A number of rather small gods, then, should haunt us today – I would call them fairies if the word were not consecrated to imbecility. (Do you believe in fairies? No, not under any circumstances.) The stuff of daily life will be tugged and strained in various directions, the earth will be given little tilts, mischievous or pensive, spotlights will fall on objects that have no reason to anticipate or welcome them, and tragedy herself, though not excluded, will have a fortuitous air as if a word would disarm her. The power of fantasy penetrates into every corner of the universe, but not into the forces that govern it – the stars that are the brain of heaven, the army of unalterable law, remain untouched – and novels of this type have an improvised air, which is the secret of their force and charm. They may contain solid character-drawing, penetrating and bitter criticism of conduct and civilization; yet our simile of the beam of light must remain, and if one god must be invoked specially let us call upon Hermes – messenger, thief, and conductor of souls to a not too terrible hereafter.

You will expect me now to say that a fantastic book asks us to accept the supernatural. I will say it, but reluctantly, because any statement as to their subject-matter brings these novels into the claws of critical apparatus, from which it is important that they should be saved. It is truer of them than of most books that we can only know what is in them by reading them, and their appeal is specially personal – they are side-shows inside the main show. So I would rather hedge as much as possible, and say that they ask us to accept either the supernatural or its absence.

A reference to the greatest of them – *Tristram Shandy* – will make this point clear. The supernatural is absent from the Shandy ménage, yet a thousand incidents suggest that it is not far off. It would not be really odd, would it, if the furniture in Mr Shandy's bedroom, where he retired in despair after hearing the omitted details of his son's birth, should come alive like Belinda's toilette in *The Rape of the Lock*, or that Uncle Toby's drawbridge should lead into Lilliput? There is a charmed stagnation about the whole epic – the more the characters do the less gets done, the less they have to say the more they talk, the harder they think the softer they get, facts have an unholy tendency to unwind and trip up the past instead of begetting the future, as in well-conducted books, and the obstinacy of inanimate objects, like Dr Slop's bag, is most suspicious. Obviously a god is hidden in *Tristram Shandy*, his name is Muddle, and some readers cannot accept him. Muddle is almost incarnate – quite to reveal his awful features was not Sterne's intention; that is the deity that lurks behind his masterpiece – the army of unutterable muddle, the universe as a hot chestnut. Small wonder that another divine muddler, Dr Johnson, writing in 1776, should remark: 'Nothing odd will do long. *Tristram Shandy* did not last.' Dr Johnson was not always happy in his literary judgements, but the inappropriateness of this one passes belief.

Well, that must serve as our definition of fantasy. It implies the supernatural, but need not express it. Often it does express it, and were that type of classification helpful we could make a list of the devices which writers of a fantastic turn have used – such as the introduction of a god, ghost, angel, monkey, monster, midget, witch into ordinary life; or the introduction of ordinary men into no-man's-land, the future, the past, the interior of the earth, the fourth dimension; or divings into and dividings of personality; or finally the device of parody or adaptation. These devices need never grow stale; they will occur naturally to writers of a certain temperament, and be put to fresh use; but the fact that their number is strictly limited is of interest, and suggests that the beam of light can only be manipulated in certain ways.

I will select, as a typical example, a recent book about a witch: *Flecker's Magic*, by Norman Matson.[1] It seemed to me good and I recommended it to a friend whose judgement I respect. He thought it poor. That is what is so tiresome about new books: they never give us that restful feeling which we have when perusing the classics. *Flecker's Magic* contains scarcely anything that is new – fantasies cannot; only the old old story of the wishing-ring which brings either misery or nothing at all. Flecker, an American boy who is learning to paint in Paris, is given the ring by a girl in a café; she is a witch, she tells him; he has only to be sure what he wants and he will get it. To prove her power, a motor-bus rises slowly from the street and turns upside down in the air. The passengers, who do not fall out, try to look as if nothing was happening. The driver, who is standing on the pavement at the moment, cannot conceal his surprise, but when his bus returns safe to earth again he thinks it wiser to get into his seat and drive off as usual. Motor-buses do not revolve slowly through the air – so they do not. Flecker now accepts the ring. His character, though slightly sketched, is individual, and this definiteness causes the book to grip.

It proceeds with a growing tension, a series of little shocks. The method is Socratic. The boy starts by thinking of something obvious, like a Rolls Royce. But where shall he put the beastly thing? Or a beautiful lady. But what about her *carte d'identité*? Or money? Ah, that's more like it – he is almost a beggar. Say a million dollars. He prepares to turn the ring for this wish – except while one's about it two millions seem safer – or ten – or – and money blares out into madness, and the same thing happens when he thinks of long life: to die in forty years – no, in fifty – in one hundred – horrible,

1. Published by Ernest Benn.

horrible. Then a solution occurs. He has always wanted to be a great painter. Well, he'll be it at once. But what kind of greatness? Giotto's? Cézanne's? Certainly not; his own kind, and he does not know what that is, so this wish likewise is impossible.

And now a horrible old woman begins to haunt his days and dreams. She reminds him of the girl who gave the ring. She knows his thoughts and sidles up to say, 'Dear boy, darling boy! Wish for happiness!' We learn in time that she is the real witch – the girl was a human acquaintance whom she used to get into touch with Flecker. The last of the witches – very lonely. The rest have committed suicide during the eighteenth century – they could not endure to survive into the world of Newton where two and two make four, and even the world of Einstein is not sufficiently decentralized to revive them. She has hung on in the hope of smashing this world, and she wants the boy to ask for happiness because such a wish has never been made in all the history of the ring.

Perhaps Flecker was the first modern man to find himself in this predicament? The people of the old world had so little they knew surely what they wanted. They knew about Almighty God, who wore a beard and sat in an armchair about a mile above the fields, and life was very short and very long, too, for the days were so full of unthinking effort.

The people of the recorded olden times wished for a beautiful castle on a high hill and lived therein until death. But the hill was not so high one might see from the windows back along thirty centuries – as one may from a bungalow. In the castle there were no great volumes filled with words and pictures of things dug up by man's relentless curiosity from sand and soil in all corners of the world; there was a sentimental half-belief in dragons, but no knowledge that once upon a time only dragons had lived on the earth – that man's grandfather and grandmother were dragons; there were no movies flickering like thoughts against a white wall, no phonograph, no machinery with which to achieve the sensation of speed; no diagrams of the fourth dimension, no contrasts in life like that of Waterville, Minn., and Paris, France. In the castle the light was weak and flickering, hallways were dark, rooms deeply shadowed. The little outside world was full of shadow, and on the very top of the mind of him who lived in the castle played a dim light – underneath were shadows, fear, ignorance, will-to-ignorance. Most of all there was not in the castle on the hill the breathless sense of imminent revelation – that today or surely tomorrow Man would at a stroke double his power and change the world again.

The ancient tales of magic were the mumbling thoughts of a distant shabby little world – so, at least, thought Flecker, offended. The tales gave him no guidance. There was too much difference between his world and theirs . . .

He wondered if he hadn't dismissed the wish for happiness rather heedlessly? He seemed to get nowhere thinking about it. He was not wise enough. In the old tales a wish for happiness was never made! He wondered why.

He might chance it – just to see what would happen. The thought made him tremble. He leaped from his bed and paced the red-tiled floor, rubbing his hands together . . .

'I want to be happy for ever,' he whispered, to hear the words, careful not to touch the ring. '*Happy . . . for ever*' – the two syllables of the first word, like little hard pebbles, struck musically against the bell of his imagination, but the second was a sigh. *For ever* – his spirit sank under the soft, heavy impact of it. Held in his thought the word made a dreary music, fading. '*Happy . . . for ever*' – NO!!

A true fantasist, Norman Matson merges the kingdoms of magic and common sense by using words that apply to both, and the mixture he has created comes alive. I will not tell the end of the story. You will have guessed its essentials, but there are always surprises in the working of a fresh mind, and to the end of time good literature will be made round this notion of a wish.

To turn from this simple example of the supernatural to a more complicated one – to a highly accomplished and superbly written book whose spirit is farcical: *Zuleika Dobson* by Max Beerbohm. You all know Miss Dobson – not personally, or you would not be here now. She is that damsel for love of whom all the undergraduates of Oxford except one drowned themselves during Eights Week, and he threw himself out of a window.

A superb theme for a fantasy, but all will depend on the handling. It is treated with a mixture of realism, wittiness, charm and mythology, and the mythology is most important. Max has borrowed or created a number of supernatural machines – to have entrusted Zuleika to one of them would be inept; the fantasy would become heavy or thin. But we pass from the sweating emperors to the black and pink pearls, the hooting owls, the interference of the Muse Clio, the ghosts of Chopin and George Sand, of Nellie O'Mora; just as one fails another starts, to uphold this most exquisite of funeral palls.

Through the square, across the High, down Grove Street, they passed. The Duke looked up at the tower of Merton, ὡς οὔποτ' αὖθις ἀλλὰ νῦν πανύστατον. Strange that tonight it would still be standing here, in all its sober and solid beauty – still be gazing, over the roofs and chimneys, at the tower of Magdalen, its rightful bride. Through untold centuries of the future it would stand thus, gaze thus. He winced. Oxford walls have a way of belittling us; and the Duke was loth to regard his doom as trivial.

Aye, by all minerals we are mocked. Vegetables, yearly deciduous, are far more sympathetic. The lilac and laburnum, making lovely now the railed pathway to Christ Church meadow, were all a-swaying and a-nodding to the Duke as he passed by. 'Adieu, adieu, your Grace,' they were whispering. 'We are very sorry for you – very sorry indeed. We never dared suppose you would predecease us. We think your death a very great tragedy. Adieu! Perhaps we shall meet in another world – that is, if the members of the animal kingdom have immortal souls, as we have.'

The Duke was little versed in their language; yet, as he passed between these gently garrulous blooms, he caught at least the drift of their salutation, and smiled a vague but courteous acknowledgment, to the right and the left alternately, creating a very favourable impression.

Has not a passage like this a beauty unattainable by serious literature? It is funny yet charming, iridescent yet profound. Criticisms of human nature fly not like arrows but upon the wings of sylphs. Towards the end – that dreadful end often so fatal to fiction – the book rather flags: the suicide of all the undergraduates of Oxford is not as delightful as it ought to be when viewed at close quarters, and the defenestration of Noaks almost nasty. Still, it is a great work – the most consistent achievement of fantasy in our time, and the closing scene in Zuleika's bedroom with its menace of further disasters is impeccable.

And now, with pent breath and fast-beating heart, she stood staring at the lady of the mirror, without seeing her; and now she wheeled round and swiftly glided to that little table on which stood her two books. She snatched Bradshaw.

We always intervene between Bradshaw and anyone whom we see consulting him. 'Mademoiselle will permit me to find that which she seeks?' asked Mélisande.

'Be quiet,' said Zuleika. We always repulse, at first, anyone who intervenes between us and Bradshaw.

We always end by accepting the intervention. 'See if it is possible to go direct from here to Cambridge,' said Zuleika, handing the book on. 'If it isn't, then – well, see how one *does* get there.'

We never have any confidence in the intervener. Nor is the intervener, when it comes to the point, sanguine. With mistrust mounting to exasperation Zuleika sat watching the faint and frantic researches of her maid.

'Stop!' she said suddenly. 'I have a much better idea. Go down very early to the station. See the station-master. Order me a special train. For ten o'clock, say.'

Rising, she stretched her arms above her head. Her lips parted in a yawn, met in a smile. With both hands she pushed back her hair from her shoulders, and twisted it into a loose knot. Very lightly she slipped up into bed, and very soon she was asleep.

So Zuleika ought to have come on to this place. She does not seem ever to have arrived, and we can only suppose that through the intervention of the gods her special train failed to start, or, more likely, is still in a siding at Bletchley.

Among the devices in my list I mentioned 'parody' or 'adaptation' and would now examine this further. The fantasist here adopts for his mythology some earlier work, and uses it as a framework or quarry for his own purposes. There is an aborted example of this in *Joseph Andrews*. Fielding set out to use *Pamela* as a comic mythology. He thought it would be fun to invent a brother to Pamela, a pure-minded footman, who should repulse Lady Booby's attentions just as Pamela repulsed Mr B.'s, and he made Lady Booby Mr B.'s aunt. Thus he would be able to laugh at Richardson, and incidentally express his own views of life. Fielding's view of life, however, was of the sort that only rests content with the creation of solid round characters, and with the growth of Parson Adams and Mrs Slipslop the fantasy ceases, and we get an independent work. *Joseph Andrews* (which is also important historically) is interesting to us as an example of a false start. Its author begins by playing the fool in a Richardsonian world, and ends by being serious in a world of his own – the world of Tom Jones and Amelia.

Parody or adaptation have enormous advantages to certain novelists, particularly to those who may have a great deal to say and abundant literary genius, but who do not see the world in terms of individual men and women – who do not, in other words, take easily to creating characters. How are such men to start writing? An already existing book or literary tradition may inspire them – they may find high up in its cornices a pattern that will serve as a beginning, they may swing about in its rafters and gain strength. That fantasy of Lowes Dickinson, *The Magic Flute*, seems to be created thus: it has taken as its mythology the world of

Mozart. Tamino, Sarastro, and the Queen of the Night stand in their enchanted kingdom ready for the author's thoughts, and when these are poured in they become alive, and a new and exquisite work is born. And the same is true of another fantasy, anything but exquisite – James Joyce's *Ulysses*.[1] That remarkable affair – perhaps the most interesting literary experiment of our day – could not have been achieved unless Joyce had had, as his guide and butt, the world of the *Odyssey*.

I am only touching on one aspect of *Ulysses*; it is of course far more than a fantasy – it is a dogged attempt to cover the universe with mud, an inverted Victorianism, an attempt to make crossness and dirt succeed where sweetness and light failed, a simplification of the human character in the interests of Hell. All simplifications are fascinating, all lead away from the truth (which lies nearer the muddle of *Tristram Shandy*), and *Ulysses* must not detain us on the ground that it contains a morality – otherwise we shall also have to discuss Mrs Humphry Ward. We are concerned with it because, through a mythology, Joyce has been able to create the peculiar stage and characters he required.

The action of those 400,000 words occupies a single day, the scene is Dublin, the theme is a journey – the modern man's journey from morn to midnight, from bed to the squalid tasks of mediocrity, to a funeral, newspaper office, library, pub, lavatory, lying-in hospital, a saunter by the beach, brothel, coffee-stall, and so back to bed. And it coheres because it depends from the journey of a hero through the seas of Greece, like a bat hanging to a cornice.

Ulysses himself is Mr Leopold Bloom – a converted Jew –

1. *Ulysses* (Shakespeare & Co., Paris) is not at present obtainable in England. America, more enlightened, has produced a mutilated version without the author's permission and without paying him a cent. [Complete and authorized editions were first published in the U.S.A. in 1934 and in Britain in 1936.]

greedy, lascivious, timid, undignified, desultory, superficial, kindly, and always at his lowest when he pretends to aspire. He tries to explore life through the body. Penelope is Mrs Marion Bloom, an overblown soprano, by no means harsh to her suitors. The third character is young Stephen Dedalus, whom Bloom recognizes as his spiritual son much as Ulysses recognizes Telemachus as his actual son. Stephen tries to explore life through the intellect – we have met him before in *A Portrait of the Artist as a Young Man*, and now he is worked into this epic of grubbiness and disillusion. He and Bloom meet halfway through in Night Town (which corresponds partly to Homer's Palace of Circe, partly to his Descent into Hell), and in its supernatural and filthy alleys they strike up their slight but genuine friendship. This is the crisis of the book, and here – and indeed throughout – smaller mythologies swarm and pullulate, like vermin between the scales of a poisonous snake. Heaven and earth fill with infernal life, personalities melt, sexes interchange, until the whole universe, including poor, pleasure-loving Mr Bloom, is involved in one joyless orgy.

Does it come off? No, not quite. Indignation in literature never quite comes off either in Juvenal or Swift or Joyce; there is something in words that is alien to its simplicity. The Night Town scene does not come off except as a superfetation of fantasies, a monstrous coupling of reminiscences. Such satisfaction as can be attained in this direction is attained, and all through the book we have similar experiments – the aim of which is to degrade all things, and more particularly civilization and art, by turning them inside out and upside down. Some enthusiasts may think that *Ulysses* ought to be mentioned not here but later on, under the heading of prophecy, and I understand this criticism. But I prefer to mention it here with *Tristram Shandy*, *Flecker's Magic*, *Zuleika Dobson* and *The Magic Flute*, because the raging of Joyce, like the happier or calmer moods of the other writers, seems essentially fantastic, and lacks the note for which we shall be listening soon.

We must pursue this notion of mythology further, and more circumspectly.

7

PROPHECY

WITH prophecy in the narrow sense of foretelling the future
we have no concern, and we have not much concern with it
as an appeal for righteousness. What will interest us today –
what we must respond to, for interest now becomes an in-
appropriate word – is an accent in the novelist's voice, an
accent for which the flutes and saxophones of fantasy may
have prepared us. His theme is the universe, or something
universal, but he is not necessarily going to 'say' anything
about the universe; he proposes to sing, and the strangeness
of song arising in the halls of fiction is bound to give us a
shock. How will song combine with the furniture of common
sense? we shall ask ourselves, and shall have to answer 'Not
too well': the singer does not always have room for his
gestures, the tables and chairs get broken, and the novel
through which bardic influence has passed often has a
wrecked air, like a drawing-room after an earthquake or a
children's party. Readers of D. H. Lawrence will understand what I mean.

Prophecy – in our sense – is a tone of voice. It may imply
any of the faiths that have haunted humanity – Christianity,
Buddhism, dualism, Satanism, or the mere raising of human
love and hatred to such a power that their normal recep-
tacles no longer contain them; but what particular view of
the universe is recommended – with that we are not directly
concerned. It is the implication that signifies and will filter
into the turns of the novelist's phrase, and in this lecture,
which promises to be so vague and grandiose, we may come
nearer than elsewhere to the minutiae of style. We shall
have to attend to the novelist's state of mind and to the

actual words he uses; we shall neglect as far as we can the problems of common sense. As far as we can: for all novels contain tables and chairs, and most readers of fiction look for them first. Before we condemn him for affectation and distortion we must realize his viewpoint. He is not looking at the tables and chairs at all, and that is why they are out of focus. We only see what he does not focus – not what he does – and in our blindness we laugh at him.

I have said that each aspect of the novel demands a different quality in the reader. Well, the prophetic aspect demands two qualities: humility and the suspension of the sense of humour. Humility is a quality for which I have only a limited admiration. In many phases of life it is a great mistake and degenerates into defensiveness or hypocrisy. But humility is in place just now. Without its help we shall not hear the voice of the prophet, and our eyes will behold a figure of fun instead of his glory. And the sense of humour – that is out of place; that estimable adjunct of the educated man must be laid aside. Like the schoolchildren in the Bible, one cannot help laughing at a prophet – his bald head is so absurd – but one can discount the laughter and realize that it has no critical value and is merely food for bears.

Let us distinguish between the prophet and the non-prophet.

There were two novelists, who were both brought up in Christianity. They speculated and broke away, yet they neither left nor did they want to leave the Christian spirit, which they interpreted as a loving spirit. They both held that sin is always punished, and punishment a purgation, and they saw this process not with the detachment of an ancient Greek or a modern Hindu, but with tears in their eyes. Pity, they felt, is the atmosphere in which morality exercises its logic, a logic which otherwise is crude and meaningless. What is the use of a sinner being punished and cured if there is not an addition in the cure, a heavenly bonus? And where does the addition come from? Not out of the machinery, but out of the atmosphere in which the process occurs, out of the love and pity which (they believed) are attributes of God.

How similar these two novelists must have been! Yet one of them was George Eliot and the other Dostoyevsky.

It will be said that Dostoyevsky had vision. Still, so had George Eliot. To classify them apart – and they must be parted – is not so easy. But the difference between them will define itself at once exactly if I read two passages from their works. To the classifier the passages will seem similar; to anyone who has an ear for song they come out of different worlds.

I will begin with a passage – fifty years ago it was a very famous passage – out of *Adam Bede*. Hetty is in prison, condemned to die for the murder of her illegitimate child. She will not confess, she is hard and impenitent. Dinah, the Methodist, comes to visit her.

> Dinah began to doubt whether Hetty was conscious who it was that sat beside her ... But she felt the Divine presence more and more, – nay, as if she herself were a part of it, and it was the Divine pity that was beating in her heart, and was willing the rescue of this helpless one. At last she was prompted to speak, and find out how far Hetty was conscious of the present.
>
> 'Hetty,' she said gently, 'do you know who it is that sits by your side?'
>
> 'Yes,' Hetty answered slowly, 'it's Dinah.' ... Then, after a pause, she added, 'But you can do nothing for me. You can't make 'em do anything. They'll hang me o' Monday – it's Friday now.' ...
>
> 'But Hetty, there is some one else in this cell besides me, some one close to you.'
>
> Hetty said, in a frightened whisper, 'Who?'
>
> 'Some one who has been with you through all your hours of sin and trouble – who has known every thought you have had – has seen where you went, where you lay down and rose up again, and

all the deeds you have tried to hide in darkness. And on Monday, when I can't follow you, – when my arms can't reach you, – when death has parted us, – He who is with us now, and knows all, will be with you then. It makes no difference – whether we live or die, we are in the presence of God.'

'Oh, Dinah, won't nobody do anything for me? *Will* they hang me for certain? ... I wouldn't mind if they'd let me live ... help me ... I can't feel anything like you ... my heart is hard.'

Dinah held the clinging hand, and all her soul went forth in her voice:

'... Come, mighty Saviour! let the dead hear Thy voice; let the eyes of the blind be opened: let her see that God encompasses her; let her tremble at nothing but at the sin that cuts her off from Him. Melt the hard heart; unseal the closed lips: make her cry with her whole soul, "Father, I have sinned." ...'

'Dinah,' Hetty sobbed out, throwing her arms round Dinah's neck, 'I will speak ... I will tell ... I won't hide it any more ... I did do it, Dinah ... I buried it in the wood ... the little baby ... and it cried ... I heard it cry ... ever such a way off ... all night ... and I went back because it cried.'

She paused, and then spoke hurriedly in a louder pleading tone.

'But I thought perhaps it wouldn't die – there might somebody find it. I didn't kill it – I didn't kill it myself. I put it down there and covered it up, and when I came back it was gone ... I don't know what I felt till I saw the baby was gone. And when I'd put it there, I thought I should like somebody to find it, and save it from dying; but when I saw it was gone, I was struck like a stone, with fear. I never thought o' stirring, I felt so weak. I knew I couldn't run away, and everybody as saw me 'ud know about the baby. My heart went like a stone: I couldn't wish or try for anything; it seemed like as if I should stay there for ever, and nothing 'ud ever change. But they came and took me away.'

Hetty was silent, but she shuddered again, as if there was still something behind; and Dinah waited, for her heart was so full, that tears must come before words. At last Hetty burst out, with a sob,

'Dinah, do you think God will take away that crying and the place in the wood, now I've told everything?'

'Let us pray, poor sinner: let us fall on our knees again, and pray to the God of all mercy.'

I have not done justice to this scene, because I have had to cut it, and it is on her massiveness that George Eliot depends – she has no nicety of style. The scene is sincere, solid, pathetic, and penetrated with Christianity. The God whom Dinah summons is a living force to the authoress also; he is not brought in to work up the reader's feelings; he is the natural accompaniment of human error and suffering.

Now contrast with it the following scene from *The Brothers Karamazov* (Mitya is being accused of the murder of his father; he is spiritually though not technically guilty).

They proceeded to a final revision of the protocol. Mitya got up, moved from his chair to the corner by the curtain, lay down on a large chest covered by a rug, and instantly fell asleep.

He had a strange dream, utterly out of keeping with the place and the time.

He was driving somewhere in the steppes, where he had been stationed long ago, and a peasant was driving him in a cart with a pair of horses, through snow and sleet . . . Not far off was a village, he could see the black huts, and half the huts were burnt down, there were only the charred beams sticking up. And as they drove in, there were peasant women drawn up along the road, a lot of women, a whole row, all thin and wan, with their faces a sort of brownish colour, especially one at the edge, a tall, bony woman, who looked forty, but might have been only twenty, with a long thin face. And in her arms was a little baby crying. And her breasts seemed so dried up that there was not a drop of milk in them. And the child cried and cried, and held out its little bare arms, with its little fists blue from cold.

'Why are they crying? Why are they crying?' Mitya asked as they dashed gaily by.

'It's the babe,' answered the driver, 'the babe weeping.'

And Mitya was struck by his saying, in his peasant way, 'the babe', and he liked the peasant's calling it a 'babe'. There seemed more pity in it.

'But why is it weeping?' Mitya persisted stupidly, 'why are its little arms bare? Why don't they wrap it up?' . . .

'Why, they're poor people, burnt out. They've no bread. They're begging because they've been burnt out.'

'No, no,' Mitya, as it were, still did not understand. 'Tell me why it is those poor mothers stand there? Why are people poor? Why is the babe poor? Why is the steppe barren? Why don't they hug each other and kiss? Why don't they sing songs of joy? Why are they so dark from black misery? Why don't they feed the babe?'

And he felt that, though his questions were unreasonable and senseless, yet he wanted to ask just that, and he had to ask it just in that way. And he felt that a passion of pity, such as he had never known before, was rising in his heart, that he wanted to cry, that he wanted to do something for them all, so that the babe should weep no more, so that the dark-faced, dried-up mother should not weep, that no one should shed tears again from that moment, and he wanted to do it at once, at once, regardless of all obstacles, with all the recklessness of the Karamazovs . . . And his heart glowed, and he struggled forward towards the light, and he longed to live, to live, to go on and on, towards the new, beckoning light, and to hasten, hasten, now, at once!

'What! Where?' he exclaimed, opening his eyes, and sitting up on the chest, as though he had revived from a swoon, smiling brightly. Nikolay Parfenovitch was standing over him, suggesting that he should hear the protocol read aloud and sign it. Mitya guessed that he had been asleep an hour or more, but he did not hear Nikolay Parfenovitch. He was suddenly struck by the fact that there was a pillow under his head, which hadn't been there when he had leant back, exhausted, on the chest.

'Who put that pillow under my head? Who was so kind?' he cried, with a sort of ecstatic gratitude, and tears in his voice, as though some great kindness had been shown him.

He never found out who this kind man was, perhaps one of the peasant witnesses, or Nikolay Parfenovitch's little secretary had compassionately thought to put a pillow under his head, but his whole soul was quivering with tears. He went to the table and said that he would sign whatever they liked.

'I've had a good dream, gentlemen,' he said in a strange voice, with a new light, as of joy, in his face.

Now the difference between these passages is that the first writer is a preacher, and the second a prophet. George Eliot talks about God, but never alters her focus; God and the tables and chairs are all in the same plane, and in consequence we have not for a moment the feeling that the whole universe needs pity and love – they are only needed in Hetty's cell. In Dostoyevsky the characters and situations always stand for more than themselves; infinity attends them, though they remain individuals they expand to embrace it and summon it to embrace them; one can apply to them the saying of St Catherine of Siena that God is in the soul and the soul is in God as the sea is in the fish and the fish is in the sea. Every sentence he writes implies this extension, and the implication is the dominant aspect of his work. He is a great novelist in the ordinary sense – that is to say, his characters have relation to ordinary life and also live in their own surroundings, there are incidents which keep us excited, and so on; he has also the greatness of a prophet, to which our ordinary standards are inapplicable.

That is the gulf between Hetty and Mitya, though they inhabit the same moral and mythological worlds. Hetty, taken by herself, is quite adequate. She is a poor girl, brought to confess her crime, and so to a better frame of mind. But Mitya, taken by himself, is not adequate. He only becomes real through what he implies, his mind is not in a frame at all. Taken by himself he seems distorted out of drawing, intermittent; we begin explaining him away and saying he was disproportionately grateful for the pillow because he was overwrought – very like a Russian in fact. We cannot understand him until we see that he extends, and that the part of him on which Dostoyevsky focused did not lie on that wooden chest or even in dreamland, but in a region where it could be joined by the rest of humanity. Mitya is – all of us. So is Alyosha, so is Smerdyakov. He is the prophetic vision, and the novelist's creation also. He does not become all of us here; he is Mitya here as Hetty is Hetty. The extension, the melting, the unity through love and pity occur in a region which can only be implied, and to which fiction is perhaps the wrong approach. The world of the Karamazovs and Myshkin and Raskolnikov, the world of Moby Dick which we shall enter shortly – it is not a veil, it is not an allegory. It is the ordinary world of fiction, but it reaches back. And that tiny humorous figure of Lady Bertram whom we considered some time ago – Lady Bertram sitting on her sofa with pug – may assist us in these deeper matters. Lady Bertram, we decided, was a flat character, capable of extending into a round when the action required it. Mitya is a round character, but he too is capable of extension. He does not conceal anything (mysticism), he does not mean anything (symbolism), he is merely Dmitri Karamazov, but to be merely a person in Dostoyevsky is to join up with all the other people far back. Consequently the tremendous current suddenly flows – for me in those closing words: 'I've had a good dream, gentlemen.' Have I had that good dream too? No. Dostoyevsky's characters ask us to share something deeper than their experiences. They convey to us a sensation that is partly physical – the sensation of sinking into a translucent globe and seeing our experience floating far above us on its surface, tiny, remote, yet ours. We have not ceased to be people, we have given nothing up, but 'the sea is in the fish and the fish is in the sea'.

There we touch the limit of our subject. We are not concerned with the prophet's message, or rather (if matter and manner cannot be separated) we are concerned with it as little as possible. What matters is the accent of his voice, his song. Hetty might have a good dream in prison, and it would be true of her, satisfyingly true, but it would stop short. Dinah would say she was glad, Hetty would recount her dream, which, unlike Mitya's, would be logically connected with the crisis, and George Eliot would say something sound and sympathetic about good dreams generally, and their inexplicably helpful effect on the tortured breast. Just the same and absolutely different are the two scenes, the two books, the two writers.

Now another point emerges. Regarded merely as a novelist, the prophet has certain uncanny advantages, so that it is sometimes worth letting him into a drawing-room even on the furniture's account. Perhaps he will smash or distort, but perhaps he will illumine. As I said of the fantasist, he manipulates a beam of light which occasionally touches the objects so sedulously dusted by the hand of common sense, and renders them more vivid than they can ever be in domesticity. This intermittent realism pervades all the greater works of Dostoyevsky and Herman Melville. Dostoyevsky can be patiently accurate about a trial or the appearance of a staircase. Melville can catalogue the products of the whale ('I have ever found your plain things the knottiest of all,' he remarks). D. H. Lawrence can describe a field of grass and flowers or the entrance into Freemantle. Little things in the foreground seem to be all that the prophet cares about at moments – he sits down with them so quiet and busy, like a child between two romps. What does he feel during these intermittencies? Is it another form of excitement, or is he resting? We cannot know. No doubt it is what A. E. feels when he is doing his creameries, or what Claudel feels when he is doing his diplomacy, but what is that? Anyhow, it characterizes these novels and gives them what is always provocative in a work of art: roughness of surface. While they pass under our eyes they are full of dents and grooves and lumps and spikes which draw from us little cries of approval and disapproval. When they have passed, the roughness is forgotten, they become as smooth as the moon.

Prophetic fiction, then, seems to have definite characteristics. It demands humility and the absence of the sense of humour. It reaches back – though we must not conclude from the example of Dostoyevsky that it always reaches back to pity and love. It is spasmodically realistic. And it gives us the sensation of a song or of sound. It is unlike fantasy because its face is towards unity, whereas fantasy glances about. Its confusion is incidental, whereas fantasy's is fundamental – *Tristram Shandy* ought to be a muddle, *Zuleika Dobson* ought to keep changing mythologies. Also the prophet – one imagines – has gone 'off' more completely than the fantasist, he is in a remoter emotional state while he composes. Not many novelists have this aspect. Poe is too incidental. Hawthorne potters too anxiously round the problem of individual salvation to get free. Hardy, a philosopher and a great poet, might seem to have claims, but Hardy's novels are surveys; they do not give out sounds. The writer sits back, it is true, but the characters do not reach back. He shows them to us as they let their arms rise and fall in the air; they may parallel our sufferings but can never extend them – never, I mean, could Jude step forward like Mitya and release floods of our emotion by saying, 'Gentlemen, I've had a bad dream.' Conrad is in a rather similar position. The voice, the voice of Marlow, is too full of experiences to sing, it is dulled by many reminiscences of error and beauty, its owner has seen too much to see beyond cause and effect. To have a philosophy – even a poetic and emotional philosophy like Hardy's and Conrad's – leads to reflections on life and things. A prophet does not reflect. And he does not hammer away. That is why we exclude Joyce. Joyce has many qualities akin to prophecy and he has shown (especially in the *Portrait of the Artist*) an imaginative grasp of evil. But he undermines the universe in too workmanlike a manner, looking round for this tool or that; in spite of all his internal looseness he is too tight, he is never vague except after due deliberation; it is talk, talk, never song.

So, though I believe this lecture is on a genuine aspect of the novel, not a fake aspect, I can only think of four writers to illustrate it – Dostoyevsky, Melville, D. H. Lawrence and Emily Brontë. Emily Brontë shall be left to the last, Dostoyevsky I have alluded to, Melville is the centre of our picture, and the centre of Melville is *Moby Dick*.

Moby Dick is an easy book, as long as we read it as a yarn or an account of whaling interspersed with snatches of poetry. But, as soon as we catch the song in it, it grows difficult and immensely important. Narrowed and hardened into words, the spiritual theme of *Moby Dick* is as follows: a battle against evil, conducted too long or in the wrong way. The White Whale is evil, and Captain Ahab is warped by constant pursuit until his knight-errantry turns into revenge. These are words – a symbol for the book if we want one – but they do not carry us much further than the acceptance of the book as a yarn – perhaps they carry us backwards, for they may mislead us into harmonizing the incidents, and so losing their roughness and richness. The idea of a contest we may retain: all action is a battle, the only happiness is peace. But contest between what? We get false if we say that it is between good and evil, or between two unreconciled evils. The essential in *Moby Dick*, its prophetic song, flows athwart the action and the surface morality like an undercurrent. It lies outside words. Even at the end, when the ship has gone down with the bird of heaven pinned to its mast, and the empty coffin, bouncing up from the vortex, has carried Ishmael back to the world – even then we cannot catch the words of the song. There has been stress, with intervals; but no explicable solution, certainly no reaching back into universal pity and love; no 'Gentlemen, I've had a good dream'.

The extraordinary nature of the book appears in two of its early incidents – the sermon about Jonah and the friendship with Queequeg.

The sermon has nothing to do with Christianity. It asks for endurance or loyalty without hope of reward. The preacher, 'kneeling in the pulpit's bows, folded his large brown hands across his chest, uplifted his closed eyes, and offered a prayer so deeply devout that he seemed kneeling and praying at the bottom of the sea'. And he concludes on a note of joy more terrifying than a menace:

Delight is to him whose strong arms yet support him, when the ship of this base treacherous world has gone down beneath him. Delight is to him, who gives no quarter in the truth, and kills, burns, and destroys all sin though he pluck it out from under the robes of Senators and Judges. Delight, – top-gallant delight is to him, who acknowledges no law or lord, but the Lord his God, and is only a patriot to heaven. Delight is to him, whom all the waves of the billows of the seas of the boisterous mob can never shake from this sure Keel of the Ages. And eternal delight and deliciousness will be his, who coming to lay him down, can say with his final breath – O Father! – chiefly known to me by Thy rod – mortal or immortal, here I die. I have striven to be Thine, more than to be this world's, or mine own. Yet this is nothing: I leave eternity to Thee; for what is man that he should live out the lifetime of his God?

I believe it is not a coincidence that the last ship we encounter at the end of the book before the final catastrophe should be called the Delight; a vessel of ill omen who has herself encountered Moby Dick and been shattered by him. But what the connection was in the prophet's mind I cannot say, nor could he tell us.

Immediately after the sermon, Ishmael makes a passionate alliance with the cannibal Queequeg, and it looks for a

moment that the book is to be a saga of blood-brotherhood.
But human relationships mean little to Melville, and after a
grotesque and violent entry Queequeg is almost forgotten.
Almost – not quite. Towards the end he falls ill, and a coffin
is made for him which he does not occupy, as he recovers.
It is this coffin, serving as a life-buoy, that saves Ishmael
from the final whirlpool, and this again is no coincidence,
but an unformulated connection that sprang up in Melville's
mind. *Moby Dick* is full of meanings; its meaning is a different problem. It is wrong to turn the Delight or the coffin
into symbols, because even if the symbolism is correct it
silences the book. Nothing can be stated about *Moby Dick*
except that it is a contest. The rest is song.

It is to his conception of evil that Melville's work owes
much of its strength. As a rule, evil has been feebly envisaged in fiction, which seldom soars above misconduct or
avoids the clouds of mysteriousness. Evil to most novelists
is either sexual and social, or something very vague for
which a special style with implications of poetry is thought
suitable. They want it to exist, in order that it may kindly
help them on with the plot, and evil, not being kind, generally hampers them with a villain – a Lovelace or Uriah
Heep, who does more harm to the author than to the fellow
characters. For a real villain we must turn to a story of
Melville's called *Billy Budd*.[1]

It is a short story, but must be mentioned because of the
light it throws on his other work. The scene is a British
man-of-war soon after the mutiny at the Nore – a stagy yet
intensely real vessel. The hero, a handsome young sailor,
has goodness of the glowing aggressive sort which cannot
exist unless it has evil to consume. He is not himself aggressive. It is the light within him that irritates and explodes.

1. Only to be found in the collected edition. For knowledge of it, and
for much else, I am indebted to Mr John Freeman's admirable monograph on Melville.

On the surface he is a pleasant, merry, rather insensitive lad, whose perfect physique is marred by one slight defect, a stammer, which finally destroys him. He is

dropped into a world not without some man-traps and against whose subtleties simple courage . . . without any touch of defensive ugliness, is of little avail; and where such innocence as man is capable of does yet in a moral emergency not always sharpen the faculties or enlighten the will.

Claggart, one of the petty officers, at once sees in him the enemy – his own enemy, for Claggart is evil. It is again the contest between Ahab and Moby Dick, though the parts are more clearly assigned, and we are further from prophecy and nearer to morality and common sense. But not much nearer. Claggart is not like any other villain.

Natural depravity . . . has its certain negative virtues serving as silent auxiliaries . . . It is not going too far to say that it is without vices or small sins. There is a phenomenal pride in it that excludes them from anything mercenary or avaricious. In short the depravity here meant partakes nothing of the sordid or sensual. It is serious, but free from acerbity.

He accuses Billy of trying to foment a mutiny. The charge is ridiculous, yet proves fatal. For when the boy is summoned to declare his innocence he is so horrified that he cannot speak, his ludicrous stammer seizes him, the power within him explodes, and he knocks down his traducer, kills him, and has to be hanged.

Billy Budd is a remote unearthly episode, but it is a song not without words, and should be read both for its own beauty and as an introduction to more difficult works. Evil is labelled and personified instead of slipping over the ocean and round the world, and Melville's mind can be observed more easily. What one notices in him is that his apprehensions are free from personal worry, so that we become bigger, not smaller, after sharing them. He has not got that tiresome little receptacle, a conscience, which is often such a nuisance in serious writers and so contracts their effects – the conscience of Hawthorne or of Mark Rutherford. Melville – after the initial roughness of his realism – reaches straight back into the universal, to a blackness and sadness so transcending our own that they are undistinguishable from glory. He says: 'In certain moods, no man can weigh this world without throwing in something, somehow like Original Sin, to strike the uneven balance.' He threw it in, that undefinable something, the balance righted itself, and he gave us harmony and temporary salvation.

It is no wonder that D. H. Lawrence should have written two penetrating studies of Melville, for Lawrence himself is, as far as I know, the only prophetic novelist writing today – all the rest are fantasists or preachers: the only living novelist in whom the song predominates, who has the rapt bardic quality, and whom it is idle to criticize. He invites criticism because he is a preacher also – it is this minor aspect of him which makes him so difficult and misleading – an excessively clever preacher who knows how to play on the nerves of his congregation. Nothing is more disconcerting than to sit down, so to speak, before your prophet, and then suddenly to receive his boot in the pit of your stomach. 'I'm damned if I'll be humble after that,' you cry, and so lay yourself open to further nagging. Also the subject-matter of the sermon is agitating – hot denunciations or advice relating to sex – so that in the end you cannot remember whether you ought or ought not to have a body, and are only sure that you are futile. This bullying, and the honeyed sweetness which is a bully's reaction, occupy between them the foreground of Lawrence's work; his greatness lies far, far back, and rests, not like Dostoyevsky's upon Christianity, nor like Melville's upon a contest, but upon something aesthetic. The voice is Balder's voice, though the hands are the hands of Esau. The prophet is irradiating nature from within, so that every colour has a glow and every form a distinctness which could not otherwise be obtained. Take a scene that always stays in the memory: the scene in *Women in Love* where one of the characters throws stones into the water at night to shatter the image of the moon. Why he throws, what the scene symbolizes, is unimportant. But the writer could not get such a moon and water otherwise; he reaches them by his special path which stamps them as more wonderful than any we can imagine. It is the prophet back where he started from, back where the rest of us are waiting by the edge of the pool, but with a power of re-creation and evocation we shall never possess.

Humility is not easy with this irritable and irritating author, for the humbler we get the crosser he gets. Yet I do not see how else to read him. If we start resenting or mocking, his treasure disappears as surely as if we started obeying him. What is valuable about him cannot be put into words: it is colour, gesture and outline in people and things, the usual stock-in-trade of the novelist, but evolved by such a different process that they belong to a new world.

But what about Emily Brontë? Why should *Wuthering Heights* come into this enquiry? It is a story about human beings, it contains no view of the universe.

My answer is that the emotions of Heathcliff and Catherine Earnshaw function differently to other emotions in fiction. Instead of inhabiting the characters, they surround them like thunderclouds, and generate the explosions that fill the novel from the moment when Lockwood dreams of the hand at the window down to the moment when Heathcliff, with the same window open, is discovered dead. *Wuthering Heights* is filled with sound – storm and rushing wind – a sound more important than words and thoughts. Great as the novel is, one cannot afterwards remember anything in it but Heathcliff and the elder Catherine. They cause the action by their separation; they close it by their union after death. No wonder they 'walk': what else could such beings do? Even when they were alive their love and hate transcended them.

Emily Brontë had in some ways a literal and careful mind. She constructed her novel on a time-chart even more elaborate than Miss Austen's, and she arranged the Linton and Earnshaw families symmetrically, and she had a clear idea of the various legal steps by which Heathcliff gained possession of their two properties.[1] Then why did she deliberately introduce muddle, chaos, tempest? Because in our sense of the word she was a prophetess; because what is implied is more important to her than what is said; and only in confusion could the figures of Heathcliff and Catherine externalize their passion till it streamed through the house and over the moors. *Wuthering Heights* has no mythology beyond what these two characters provide; no great book is more cut off from the universals of Heaven and Hell. It is local, like the spirits it engenders, and, whereas we may meet Moby Dick in any pond, we shall only encounter them among the harebells and limestone of their own county.

A concluding remark. Always, at the back of my mind, there lurks a reservation about this prophetic stuff, a reservation which some will make more strongly while others will not make it at all. Fantasy has asked us to pay something extra, and now prophecy asks for humility and even for a suspension of the sense of humour, so that we are not allowed to snigger when a tragedy is called *Billy Budd*. We have indeed to lay aside the single vision which we bring to most of literature and life and have been trying to use through most of our enquiry, and take up a different set of tools. Is this right? Another prophet, Blake, had no doubt that it was right.

> May God us keep
> From Single vision, & Newton's sleep!

1. See that sound and brilliant essay, *The Structure of Wuthering Heights*, by C. P. S. (Hogarth Press).

he cried, and he has painted that same Newton with a pair of compasses in his hand, describing a miserable mathematical triangle and turning his back upon the gorgeous and immeasurable water-growths of *Moby Dick*. Few will agree with Blake. Fewer will agree with Blake's Newton. Most of us will be eclectics to this side or that according to our temperament. The human mind is not a dignified organ, and I do not see how we can exercise it sincerely except through eclecticism. And the only advice I would offer my fellow eclectics is: 'Do not be proud of your inconsistency. It is a pity, it is a pity that we should be equipped like this. It is a pity that Man cannot be at the same time impressive and truthful.'

For the first five lectures of this course we have used more or less the same set of tools. This time and last we have had to lay them down. Next time we shall take them up again, but with no certainty that they are the best equipment for a critic, or that there is such a thing as a critical equipment.

8

PATTERN AND RHYTHM

OUR interludes, gay and grave, are over, and we return to the general scheme of the course. We began with the story, and having considered human beings we proceeded to the plot which springs out of the story. Now we must consider something which springs mainly out of the plot, and to which the characters and any other element present also contribute. For this new aspect there appears to be no literary word – indeed the more the arts develop the more they depend on each other for definition. We will borrow, from painting first and call it the pattern. Later we will borrow from music and call it rhythm. Unfortunately both these words are vague – when people apply rhythm or pattern to literature they are apt not to say what they mean and not to finish their sentences: it is 'Oh, but surely the rhythm . . .' or 'Oh, but if you call that pattern . . .'

Before I discuss what pattern entails, and what qualities a reader must bring to its appreciation, I will give two examples of books with patterns so definite that a pictorial image sums them up: a book the shape of an hour-glass and a book the shape of a grand chain in that old-time dance, the Lancers.

Thaïs, by Anatole France, is the shape of an hour-glass.

There are two chief characters, Paphnuce the ascetic, Thaïs the courtesan. Paphnuce lives in the desert, he is saved and happy when the book starts. Thaïs leads a life of sin in Alexandria, and it is his duty to save her. In the central scene of the book they approach, he succeeds; she goes into a monastery and gains salvation, because she has met him, but he, because he has met her, is damned. The two characters converge, cross and recede with mathematical precision, and part of the pleasure we get from the book is due to this. Such is the pattern of *Thaïs* – so simple that it makes a good starting-point for a difficult survey. It is the same as the story of *Thaïs*, when events unroll in their time-sequence, and the same as the plot of *Thaïs*, when we see the two characters bound by their previous actions and taking fatal steps whose consequence they do not see. But, whereas the story appeals to our curiosity and the plot to our intelligence, the pattern appeals to our aesthetic sense, it causes us to see the book as a whole. We do not see it as an hour-glass – that is the hard jargon of the lecture-room, which must never be taken literally at this advanced stage of our enquiry. We just have a pleasure without knowing why, and when the pleasure is past, as it is now, and our minds are left free to explain it, a geometrical simile such as an hour-glass will be found helpful. If it was not for this hour-glass the story, the plot, and the characters of Thaïs and Paphnuce would none of them exert their full force, they would none of them breathe as they do. 'Pattern', which seems so rigid, is connected with atmosphere, which seems so fluid.

Now for the book that is shaped like the grand chain: *Roman Pictures* by Percy Lubbock.

Roman Pictures is a social comedy. The narrator is a tourist in Rome; he there meets a kindly and shoddy friend of his, Deering, who rebukes him superciliously for staring at churches and sets him out to explore society. This he does, demurely obedient; one person hands him on to another; café, studio, Vatican and Quirinal purlieus are all reached, until finally, at the extreme end of his career he thinks, in a most aristocratic and dilapidated palazzo, whom should he meet but the second-rate Deering; Deering is his hostess's nephew, but had concealed it owing to some backfire of snobbery. The circle is complete, the original partners have rejoined, and greet one another with mutual confusion which turns to mild laughter.

What is so good in *Roman Pictures* is not the presence of the 'grand chain' pattern – anyone can organize a grand chain – but the suitability of the pattern to the author's mood. Lubbock works all through by administering a series of little shocks, and by extending to his characters an elaborate charity which causes them to appear in a rather worse light than if no charity was wasted on them at all. It is the comic atmosphere, but sub-acid, meticulously benign. And at the end we discover to our delight that the atmosphere has been externalized, and that the partners, as they click together in the marchesa's drawing-room, have done the exact thing which the book requires, which it required from the start, and have bound the scattered incidents together with a thread woven out of their own substance.

Thaïs and *Roman Pictures* provide easy examples of pattern; it is not often that one can compare a book to a pictorial object with any accuracy, though curves, etc., are freely spoken of by critics who do not know what they want to say. We can only say (so far) that pattern is an aesthetic aspect of the novel, and that though it may be nourished by anything in the novel – any character, scene, word – it draws most of its nourishment from the plot. We noted, when discussing the plot, that it added to itself the quality of beauty, beauty a little surprised at her own arrival; that upon its neat carpentry there could be seen, by those who cared to see, the figure of the Muse; that Logic, at the moment of finishing its own house, laid the foundation of a new one. Here, here is the point where the aspect called pattern is most closely in touch with its material; here is our starting-point. It springs mainly from the plot, accompanies it like a light in the clouds, and remains visible after it has departed. Beauty is sometimes the shape of the book, the book as a whole, the unity, and our examination would be easier if it was always this. But sometimes it is not.

When it is not I shall call it rhythm. For the moment we are concerned with pattern only.

Let us examine at some length another book of the rigid type, a book with a unity, and in this sense an easy book, although it is by Henry James. We shall see in it pattern triumphant, and we shall also be able to see the sacrifices an author must make if he wants his pattern and nothing else to triumph.

The Ambassadors, like *Thaïs*, is the shape of an hour-glass. Strether and Chad, like Paphnuce and Thaïs, change places, and it is the realization of this that makes the book so satisfying at the close. The plot is elaborate and subtle, and proceeds by action or conversation or meditation through every paragraph. Everything is planned, everything fits: none of the minor characters are just decorative like the talkative Alexandrians at Nicias' banquet; they elaborate on the main theme, they work. The final effect is pre-arranged, dawns gradually on the reader, and is completely successful when it comes. Details of the intrigue may be forgotten, but the symmetry created is enduring.

Let us trace the growth of this symmetry.[1]

Strether, a sensitive middle-aged American, is commissioned by his old friend, Mrs Newsome, whom he hopes to marry, to go to Paris and rescue her son Chad, who has gone to the bad in that appropriate city. The Newsomes are sound commercial people, who have made money over manufacturing a small article of domestic utility. Henry James never tells us what the small article is, and in a moment we shall understand why. Wells spits it out in *Tono-Bungay*, Meredith reels it out in *Evan Harrington*, Trollope prescribes it freely for Miss Dunstable, but for James to indicate how his characters made their pile – it would not do. The article is somewhat ignoble and ludicrous

1. There is a masterly analysis of *The Ambassadors* from another standpoint in *The Craft of Fiction*.

– that is enough. If you choose to be coarse and daring and visualize it for yourself as, say, a button-hook, you can, but you do so at your own risk; the author remains uninvolved.

Well, whatever it is, Chad Newsome ought to come back and help make it, and Strether undertakes to fetch him. He has to be rescued from a life which is both immoral and unremunerative.

Strether is a typical James character – he recurs in nearly all the books and is an essential part of their construction. He is the observer who tries to influence the action, and who through his failure to do so gains extra opportunities for observation. And the other characters are such as an observer like Strether is capable of observing – through lenses procured from a rather too first-class oculist. Everything is adjusted to his vision, yet he is not a quietist – no, that is the strength of the device; he takes us along with him, we move.

When he lands in England (and a landing is an exalted and enduring experience for James, it is as vital as Newgate for Defoe; poetry and life crowd round a landing) – when Strether lands, though it is only old England, he begins to have doubts of his mission, which increase when he gets to Paris. For Chad Newsome, far from going to the bad, has improved: he is distinguished, he is so sure of himself that he can be kind and cordial to the man who has orders to fetch him away; his friends are exquisite, and as for 'women in the case' whom his mother anticipated, there is no sign of them whatever. It is Paris that has enlarged and redeemed him – and how well Strether himself understands this!

His greatest uneasiness seemed to peep at him out of the possible impression that almost any acceptance of Paris might give one's authority away. It hung before him this morning, the vast bright Babylon, like some huge iridescent object, a jewel brilliant and hard, in which parts were not to be discriminated nor differences

comfortably marked. It twinkled and trembled and melted together; and what seemed all surface one moment seemed all depth
the next. It was a place of which, unmistakably, Chad was fond;
wherefore, if he, Strether, should like it too much, what on earth,
with such a bond, would become of either of them?

Thus, exquisitely and firmly, James sets his atmosphere –
Paris irradiates the book from end to end, it is an actor
though always unembodied, it is a scale by which human
sensibility can be measured, and when we have finished the
novel, and allow its incidents to blur that we may see the
pattern plainer, it is Paris that gleams at the centre of the
hour-glass shape – Paris – nothing so crude as good or evil.
Strether sees this, and sees that Chad sees it, and when this
stage is reached the novel takes a turn: there is, after all, a
woman in the case: behind Paris, interpreting it for Chad,
is the adorable and exalted figure of Mme de Vionnet. It is
now impossible for Strether to proceed. All that is noble and
refined in life concentrates in Mme de Vionnet and is reinforced by her pathos. She asks him not to take Chad away.
He promises – without reluctance, for his own heart has
already shown him as much – and he remains in Paris not
to fight it but to fight for it.

For the second batch of ambassadors now arrives from
the New World. Mrs Newsome, incensed and puzzled by
the unseemly delay, has dispatched Chad's sister, his
brother-in-law and Mamie, the girl whom he is supposed
to marry. The novel now becomes, within its ordained
limits, most amusing. There is a superb set-to between the
sister and Mme de Vionnet, while as for Mamie – here is
Mamie, seen through Strether's eyes.

As a child, as a 'bud', and then again as a flower of expansion,
Mamie had bloomed for him, freely, in the almost incessantly
open doorways of home; where he remembered her as first very
forward, as then very backward – for he had carried on at one
period, in Mrs Newsome's parlours ... a course of English

ASPECTS OF THE NOVEL

literature reinforced by exams and teas – and once more, finally,
as very much in advance. But he had kept no great sense of points
of contact; it not being in the nature of things at Woollett that the
freshest of the buds should find herself in the same basket with the
most withered of the winter apples . . . He none the less felt, as he
sat with the charming girl, the signal growth of a confidence. For
she *was* charming, when all was said – and none the less so for the
visible habit and practice of freedom and fluency. She was charming, he was aware, in spite of the fact that if he hadn't found her
so he would have found her something he should have been in
peril of expressing as 'funny'. Yes, she was funny, wonderful
Mamie, and without dreaming it; she was bland, she was bridal –
with never, that he could make out as yet, a bridegroom to support
it; she was handsome and portly and easy and chatty, soft and
sweet and almost disconcertingly reassuring. She was dressed, if
we might so far discriminate, less as a young lady than as an old
one – had an old one been supposable to Strether as so committed
to vanity; the complexities of her hair missed moreover also the
looseness of youth; and she had a mature manner of bending a
little, as to encourage and reward, while she held neatly together
in front of her a pair of strikingly polished hands: the combination
of all of which kept up about her the glamour of her 'receiving',
placed her again perpetually between the windows and within
sound of the ice-cream plates, suggested the enumeration of all
the names . . . gregarious specimens of a single type, she was happy
to 'meet'.

Mamie is another Henry James type; nearly every novel
contains her – Mrs Gereth in *The Spoils of Poynton* for instance, or Henrietta Stackpole in *The Portrait of a Lady*. He
is so good at indicating instantaneously and constantly that
a character is second-rate, deficient in sensitiveness, abounding in the wrong sort of worldliness; he gives such characters
so much vitality that their absurdity is delightful.

So Strether changes sides and loses all hopes of marrying
Mrs Newsome. Paris is winning – and then he catches sight
of something new. Is not Chad, as regards any fineness in
him, played out? Is not Chad's Paris after all just a place

for a spree? This fear is confirmed. He goes for a solitary country walk, and at the end of the day he comes across Chad and Mme de Vionnet. They are in a boat, they pretend not to see him, because their relation is at bottom an ordinary liaison, and they are ashamed. They were hoping for a secret week-end at an inn while their passion survived; for it will not survive, Chad will tire of the exquisite Frenchwoman, she is part of his fling; he will go back to his mother and make the little domestic article and marry Mamie. They know all this, and it is revealed to Strether though they try to hide it; they lie, they are vulgar – even Mme de Vionnet, even her pathos, is stained with commonness.

It was like a chill in the air to him, it was almost appalling, that a creature so fine could be, by mysterious forces, a creature so exploited. For, at the end of all things, they *were* mysterious; she had but made Chad what he was – so why could she think she had made him infinite? She had made him better, she had made him best, she had made him anything one would; but it came to our friend with supreme queerness that he was none the less only Chad ... The work, however admirable, was nevertheless of the strict human order, and in short it was marvellous that the companion of mere earthly joys, of comforts, aberrations – however one classed them – within the common experience, should be so transcendently prized ...

She was older for him tonight, visibly less exempt from the touch of time; but she was as much as ever the finest and subtlest creature, the happiest apparition, it had been given him, in all his years, to meet; and yet he could see her there as vulgarly troubled, in very truth, as a maidservant crying for her young man. The only thing was that she judged herself as the maidservant wouldn't; the weakness of which wisdom too, the dishonour of which judgement, seemed but to sink her lower.

So Strether loses them too. As he says: 'That, you see, is my only logic. Not, out of the whole affair, to have got anything for myself.' It is not that they have gone back. It is that he has gone on. The Paris they revealed to him – he could reveal it to them now, if they had eyes to see, for it is something finer than they could ever notice for themselves, and his imagination has more spiritual value than their youth. The pattern of the hour-glass is complete: he and Chad have changed places, with more subtle steps than Thaïs and Paphnuce, and the light in the clouds proceeds not from the well-lit Alexandria, but from the jewel which 'twinkled and trembled and melted together; and what seemed all surface one moment seemed all depth the next'.

The beauty that suffuses *The Ambassadors* is the reward due to a fine artist for hard work. James knew exactly what he wanted, he pursued the narrow path of aesthetic duty, and success to the full extent of his possibilities has crowned him. The pattern has woven itself, with modulation and re-servations Anatole France will never attain. But at what sacrifice!

So enormous is the sacrifice that many readers cannot get interested in James, although they can follow what he says (his difficulty has been much exaggerated), and can appre-ciate his effects. They cannot grant his premise, which is that most of human life has to disappear before he can do us a novel.

He has, in the first place, a very short list of characters. I have already mentioned two – the observer who tries to influence the action, and the second-rate outsider (to whom, for example, all the brilliant opening of *What Maisie Knew* is entrusted). Then there is the sympathetic foil, very lively and frequently female – in *The Ambassadors* Maria Gostrey plays this part; there is the wonderful rare heroine, whom Mme de Vionnet approached and who is consummated by Milly in *The Wings of the Dove*; there is sometimes a villain, sometimes a young artist with generous impulses; and that is about all. For so fine a novelist it is a poor show.

In the second place, the characters, besides being few in number, are constructed on very stingy lines. They are incapable of fun, of rapid motion, of carnality and of nine-tenths of heroism. Their clothes will not take off, the diseases that ravage them are anonymous, like the sources of their income, their servants are noiseless or resemble themselves, no social explanation of the world we know is possible for them, for there are no stupid people in their world, no barriers of language and no poor. Even their sensations are limited. They can land in Europe and look at works of art and at each other, but that is all. Maimed creatures can alone breathe in Henry James's pages – maimed yet specialized. They remind one of the exquisite deformities who haunted Egyptian art in the reign of Akhnaton – huge heads and tiny legs, but nevertheless charming. In the following reign they disappear.

Now this drastic curtailment, both of the numbers of human beings and of their attributes, is in the interests of the pattern. The longer James worked, the more convinced he grew that a novel should be a whole – not necessarily geometric like *The Ambassadors*, but it should accrete round a single topic, situation, gesture, which should occupy the characters and provide a plot, and should also fasten up the novel on the outside – catch its scattered statements in a net, make them cohere like a planet, and swing through the skies of memory. A pattern must emerge, and anything that emerged from the pattern must be pruned off as wanton distraction. Who so wanton as human beings? Put Tom Jones or Emma or even Mr Casaubon into a Henry James book, and the book will burn to ashes, whereas we could put them into one another's books and only cause local in-flammation. Only a Henry James character will suit, and though they are not dead – certain selected recesses of ex-perience he explores very well – they are gutted of the common stuff that fills characters in other books, and our-selves. And this castrating is not in the interests of the Kingdom of Heaven, there is no philosophy in the novels, no religion (except an occasional touch of superstition), no prophecy, no benefit for the superhuman at all. It is for the sake of a particular aesthetic effect which is certainly gained, but at this heavy price.

H. G. Wells has been amusing on this point, and perhaps profound. In *Boon* – one of his liveliest works – he had Henry James much upon his mind, and wrote a superb parody of him.

James *begins* by taking it for granted that a novel is a work of art that must be judged by its oneness. Someone gave him that idea in the beginning of things and he has never found it out. He doesn't find things out. He doesn't even seem to want to find things out ... He accepts very readily and then – elaborates ... The only living human motives left in the novels of Henry James are a certain avidity and an entirely superficial curiosity ... His people nose out suspicions, hint by hint, link by link. Have you ever known living human beings do that? The thing his novel is *about* is always there. It is like a church lit but without a congregation to distract you, with every light and line focused on the high altar. And on the altar, very reverently placed, intensely there, is a dead kitten, an egg-shell, a bit of string ... Like his 'Altar of the Dead', with nothing to the dead at all ... For if there was they couldn't all be candles and the effect would vanish ...

Wells sent *Boon* as a present to James, apparently thinking the master would be as much pleased by such heartiness and honesty as was he himself. The master was far from pleased, and a most interesting correspondence ensued.[1] James is polite, reminiscent, bewildered, deeply outraged and ex- ceedingly formidable: he admits that the parody has not 'filled me with a fond elation', and regrets in conclusion that he can sign himself 'only yours faithfully, Henry James'. Wells is bewildered too, but in a different way; he cannot

1. See the *Letters of Henry James*, Vol. 2.

understand why the man should be upset. And, beyond the personal comedy, there is the great literary importance of the issue. It is this question of the rigid pattern: hour-glass or grand chain or converging lines of the cathedral or diverging lines of the catherine wheel, or bed of Procrustes – whatever image you like as long as it implies unity. Can it be combined with the immense richness of material which life provides? Wells and James would agree it cannot, Wells would go on to say that life should be given the preference, and must not be whittled or distended for a pattern's sake. My own prejudices are with Wells. The James novels are a unique possession, and the reader who cannot accept his premises misses some valuable and exquisite sensations. But I do not want more of his novels, especially when they are written by someone else, just as I do not want the art of Akhnaton to extend into the reign of Tutankhamen.

That then is the disadvantage of a rigid pattern. It may externalize the atmosphere, spring naturally from the plot, but it shuts the doors on life and leaves the novelist doing exercises, generally in the drawing-room. Beauty has arrived, but in too tyrannous a guise. In plays – the plays of Racine, for instance – she may be justified, because beauty can be a great empress on the stage, and reconcile us to the loss of the men we knew. But in the novel her tyranny as it grows powerful grows petty, and generates regrets which sometimes take the form of books like *Boon*. To put it in other words, the novel is not capable of as much artistic development as the drama: its humanity or the grossness of its material (use whichever phrase you like) hinder it. To most readers of fiction the sensation from a pattern is not intense enough to justify the sacrifices that made it, and their verdict is 'beautifully done, but not worth doing'.

Still, this is not the end of our quest. We will not give up the hope of beauty yet. Cannot it be introduced into fiction by some other method than the pattern? Let us edge rather nervously towards the idea of 'rhythm'.

Rhythm is sometimes quite easy. Beethoven's Fifth Symphony, for instance, starts with the rhythm 'diddidy dum', which we can all hear and tap to. But the symphony as a whole has also a rhythm – due mainly to the relation between its movements – which some people can hear but no one can tap to. This second sort of rhythm is difficult, and whether it is substantially the same as the first sort only a musician could tell us. What a literary man wants to say, though, is that the first kind of rhythm, the diddidy dum, can be found in certain novels and may give them beauty. And the other rhythm, the difficult one – the rhythm of the Fifth Symphony as a whole – I cannot quote you any parallels for that in fiction, yet it may be present.

Rhythm in the easy sense is illustrated by the work of Marcel Proust.[1]

Proust's conclusion has not been published yet, and his admirers say that when it comes everything will fall into its place, times past will be recaptured and fixed, we shall have a perfect whole. I do not believe this. The work seems to me a progressive rather than an aesthetic confession, for with the elaboration of Albertine the author is getting tired. Bits of news may await us, but it will be surprising if we have to revise our opinion of the whole book. The book is chaotic, ill-constructed, it has and will have no external shape; and yet it hangs together because it is stitched internally, because it contains rhythms.

There are several examples (the photographing of the

1. The first three books of *A la Recherche du Temps Perdu* have been excellently translated by C. K. Scott Moncrieff under the title of *Remembrance of Things Past* (Chatto & Windus). [The entire work has long been available in translation; the final volume was translated, after Scott Moncrieff's death, first (1929) by Stephen Hudson, later (1970) by Andreas Mayor.]

grandmother is one of them), but the most important, from the binding point of view, is the 'little phrase' in the music of Vinteuil. The little phrase does more than anything else – more even than the jealousy which successively destroys Swann, the hero and Charlus – to make us feel that we are in a homogeneous world. We first hear Vinteuil's name in hideous circumstances. The musician is dead – an obscure little country organist, unknown to fame – and his daughter is defiling his memory. The horrible scene is to radiate in several directions, but it passes.

Then we are at a Paris salon. A violin sonata is performed, and a little phrase from its andante catches the ear of Swann and steals into his life. It is always a living being, but takes various forms. For a time it attends his love for Odette. The love affair goes wrong, the phrase is forgotten, we forget it. Then it breaks out again when he is ravaged by jealousy, and now it attends his misery and past happiness at once, without losing its own divine character. Who wrote the sonata? On hearing it is by Vinteuil, Swann says: 'I once knew a wretched little organist of that name – it couldn't be by him.' But it is, and Vinteuil's daughter and her friend transcribed and published it.

That seems all. The little phrase crosses the book again and again, but as an echo, a memory; we like to encounter it, but it has no binding power. Then, hundreds and hundreds of pages on, when Vinteuil has become a national possession, and there is talk of raising a statue to him in the town where he has been so wretched and so obscure, another work of his is performed – a posthumous septet. The hero listens – he is in an unknown, rather terrible universe while a sinister dawn reddens the sea. Suddenly for him, and for the reader too, the little phrase of the sonata recurs – half heard, changed, but giving complete orientation, so that he is back in the country of his childhood with the knowledge that it belongs to the unknown.

ASPECTS OF THE NOVEL

We are not obliged to agree with Proust's actual musical descriptions (they are too pictorial for my own taste), but what we must admire is his use of rhythm in literature, and his use of something which is akin by nature to the effect it has to produce – namely a musical phrase. Heard by various people – first by Swann, then by the hero – the phrase of Vinteuil is not tethered: it is not a banner such as we find George Meredith using – a double-blossomed cherry tree to accompany Clara Middleton, a yacht in smooth waters for Cecilia Halkett. A banner can only reappear, rhythm can develop, and the little phrase has a life of its own, unconnected with the lives of its auditors, as with the life of the man who composed it. It is almost an actor, but not quite, and that 'not quite' means that its power has gone towards stitching Proust's book together from the inside, and towards the establishment of beauty and the ravishing of the reader's memory. There are times when the little phrase – from its gloomy inception, through the sonata, into the septet – means everything to the reader. There are times when it means nothing and is forgotten, and this seems to me the function of rhythm in fiction: not to be there all the time like a pattern, but by its lovely waxing and waning to fill us with surprise and freshness and hope.

Done badly, rhythm is most boring, it hardens into a symbol, and instead of carrying us on it trips us up. With exasperation we find that Galsworthy's spaniel John, or whatever it is, lies under the feet again; and even Meredith's cherry trees and yachts, graceful as they are, only open the windows into poetry. I doubt that it can be achieved by the writers who plan their books beforehand, it has to depend on a local impulse when the right interval is reached. But the effect can be exquisite, it can be obtained without mutilating the characters, and it lessens our need of an external form.

That must suffice on the subject of easy rhythm in fiction:

which may be defined as repetition plus variation, and which can be illustrated by examples. Now for the more difficult question. Is there any effect in novels comparable to the effect of the Fifth Symphony as a whole, where, when the orchestra stops, we hear something that has never actually been played? The opening movement, the andante, and the trio-scherzo-trio-finale-trio-finale that composes the third block, all enter the mind at once, and extend one another into a common entity. This common entity, this new thing, is the symphony as a whole, and it has been achieved mainly (though not entirely) by the relation between the three big blocks of sound which the orchestra has been playing. I am calling this relation 'rhythmic'. If the correct musical term is something else, that does not matter; what we have now to ask ourselves is whether there is any analogy to it in fiction.

I cannot find any analogy. Yet there may be one; in music fiction is likely to find its nearest parallel.

The position of the drama is different. The drama may look towards the pictorial arts, it may allow Aristotle to discipline it, for it is not so deeply committed to the claims of human beings. Human beings have their great chance in the novel. They say to the novelist: 'Recreate us if you like, but we must come in,' and the novelist's problem, as we have seen all along, is to give them a good run and to achieve something else at the same time. Whither shall he turn? Not indeed for help but for analogy. Music, though it does not employ human beings, though it is governed by intricate laws, nevertheless does offer in its final expression a type of beauty which fiction might achieve in its own way. Expansion. That is the idea the novelist must cling to. Not completion. Not rounding off but opening out. When the symphony is over we feel that the notes and tunes composing it have been liberated, they have found in the rhythm of the whole their individual freedom. Cannot the novel be like that? Is not there something of it in *War and Peace*? – the book with which we began and in which we must end. Such an untidy book. Yet, as we read it, do not great chords begin to sound behind us, and when we have finished does not every item – even the catalogue of strategies – lead a larger existence than was possible at the time?

9

CONCLUSION

It is tempting to conclude by speculations as to the future of the novel: will it become more or less realistic, will it be killed by the cinema, and so on. Speculations, whether sad or lively, always have a large air about them, they are a convenient way of being helpful or impressive. But we have no right to entertain them. We have refused to be hampered by the past, so we must not profit by the future. We have visualized the novelists of the last two hundred years all writing together in one room, subject to the same emotions and putting the accidents of their age into the crucible of inspiration, and, whatever our results, our method has been sound – sound for an assemblage of pseudo-scholars like ourselves. But we must visualize the novelists of the next two hundred years as also writing in the room. The change in their subject-matter will be enormous; they will not change. We may harness the atom, we may land on the moon, we may abolish or intensify warfare, the mental processes of animals may be understood; but all these are trifles, they belong to history, not to art. History develops, art stands still. The novelist of the future will have to pass all the new facts through the old if variable mechanism of the creative mind.

There is, however, one question which touches our subject, and which only a psychologist could answer. But let us ask it. Will the creative process itself alter? Will the mirror get a new coat of quicksilver? In other words, can human nature change? Let us consider this possibility for a moment – we are entitled to that much relaxation.

It is amusing to listen to elderly people on this subject.

Sometimes a man says in confident tones: 'Human nature's the same in all ages. The primitive cave-man lies deep in us all. Civilization – pooh! A mere veneer. You can't alter facts.' He speaks like this when he is feeling prosperous and fat. When he is feeling depressed and is worried by the young, or is being sentimental about them on the ground that they will succeed in life when he has failed, then he will take the opposite view and say mysteriously: 'Human nature is not the same. I have seen fundamental changes in my own time. You must face facts.' And he goes on like this day after day, alternately facing facts and refusing to alter them.

All I will do is to state a possibility. If human nature does alter, it will be because individuals manage to look at themselves in a new way. Here and there people – a very few people, but a few novelists are among them – are trying to do this. Every institution and vested interest is against such a search: organized religion, the State, the family in its economic aspect, have nothing to gain, and it is only when outward prohibitions weaken that it can proceed; history conditions it to that extent. Perhaps the searchers will fail, perhaps it is impossible for the instrument of contemplation to contemplate itself, perhaps if it is possible it means the end of imaginative literature – which if I understand him rightly is the view of that acute enquirer, Mr I. A. Richards. Anyhow – that way lies movement and even combustion for the novel, for if the novelist sees himself differently he will see his characters differently, and a new system of lighting will result.

I do not know on the verge of which philosophy or what rival philosophies the above remarks are wavering, but as I look back at my own scraps of knowledge, and into my own heart, I see these two movements of the human mind: the great tedious onrush known as history, and a shy crab-like sideways movement. Both movements have been neglected in these lectures: history because it only carries people on, it is just a train full of passengers; and the crab-like movement because it is too slow and cautious to be visible over our tiny period of two hundred years. So we laid it down as an axiom when we started that human nature is unchangeable, and that it produces in rapid succession prose fictions, which fictions, when they contain 50,000 words or more, are called novels. If we had the power or licence to take a wider view, and survey all human and pre-human activity, we might not conclude like this; the crab-like movement, the shiftings of the passengers, might be visible, and the phrase 'the development of the novel' might cease to be a pseudo-scholarly tag or a technical triviality, and become important, because it implied the development of humanity.

EXTRACTS FROM FORSTER'S COMMONPLACE BOOK

Gravity

Sometimes, in his wild way of talking, he would say, that Gravity was an errant scoundrel, and he would add, – of the most dangerous kind too, – because a sly one; and that he verily believed, more honest, well-meaning people were bubbled out of their goods and money by it in one twelve-month, than by pocket-picking and shop-lifting in seven. In the naked temper which a merry heart discovered, he would say, there was no danger, – but to itself: – whereas the very essence of gravity was design, and consequently deceit; – 'twas a taught trick to gain credit of the world for more sense and knowledge than a man was worth; and that, with all its pretensions, – it was no better, but often worse, than what a *French* wit had long ago defined it, – *viz. A mysterious carriage of the body to cover the defects of the mind* . . .

– *Tristram Shandy*, 1. 11. Insight vitiated by instinct of self-defence – probably typical of Sterne, whom I have begun to read. How did he discover the art of leaving out what he did not want to say? And why was it lost again until our own time? Can nothing liberate English fiction from conscientiousness? S. clearly a great writer and his philosophy of life almost good and quite good in quotations: 'Look at little me' spoils it in the bulk.

But (now finishing *T.S.*): what character-drawing! The 'humours' or 'ruling passions' are done from within and become obsessions instead of labels. Association of ideas; psychological importance of puns. Disbelief in system:

It is a singular blessing, that nature has form'd the mind of man

with the same happy backwardness and renitency[1] against conviction, which is observed in old dogs – 'of not learning new tricks'.

What a shuttlecock of a fellow would the greatest philosopher
that ever. existed be whisk'd into at once, did he read such books,
and observe such facts, and think such thoughts, as would eternally
be making him change sides!

(Cf. *Erewhon*: 'There were some here who seemed to devote
themselves to the avoidance of every opinion with which
they were not perfectly familiar, and regarded their own
brains as a sort of sanctuary, to which if an opinion had
once resorted, none other was to attack it.')

I am convinced ... that there is a North-west passage to the
intellectual world; and that the soul of man has shorter ways of
going to work, in furnishing itself with knowledge and instruction,
than we generally take with it.

His lubricity very intelligent. Birth then – as still now – an
unexplored field for the novelist. Love a tickling feeling.
Unreality of time. Supremacy of indecision in human life.
All these make him 'modern' – cf. Proust and Joyce as well
as Butler. But he didn't take a 'view' of human life (his
sentiment only flocks of cotton wool stuck on the pulpit).

Floppy yet tenacious. His charm, when it did not subdue,
must have given the shudders.

Always a bit muddled in the head.

More I reflect on this novel the higher I place it: attempts
to read Swift, Miss Burney, Smollett, place it on a pinnacle.

More quotations from it:

Shall we be destined to the days of eternity, on holy-days, as well
as working-days, to be shewing the *relicks of learning*, as monks do
the relicks of their saints – without working one – one single
miracle with them?

1. ['Resistance to constraint or compulsion, opposition, reluctance'
(*OED*). Forster misquotes 'renitency against conviction' as 'remiss-
ness'.]

Chastity, by nature, the gentlest of all affections – give it but its head – 'tis like a ramping and a roaring lion.

'Nothing odd will do long. *Tristram Shandy* did not last,' said the unfortunate Dr Johnson in 1776.

Moll Flanders a great novel of adventure, *Peregrine Pickle* a silly one, because it was not Defoe's [*sic*] deepest impulse to tell a story. Moll physically a character, with hard plump limbs, which get into bed or pick pockets. So real that the repentance does not seem superimposed, and Defoe manages to be ribald and pious with equal sincerity. I should not have thought this possible, unless one was writing one's autobiography, or photographing someone else's. A puzzling book – gynomorphic, not one stitch of the man-made. Attractive as she is, the heroine always keeps to the rules of her game, and never tries to capture our sympathy. When she and her 'Lancashire husband' discover each other to be a penniless cheat, instead of re-criminating like [*lacuna – Forster may have been unable to remember the names of Mr and. Mrs Lammle; see the corresponding passage on pp. 65-6 and the block quotation which follows, both there and here*]. Which is both truer to life and pleasanter to read than Dickens. The couple are up against facts, not against the author's theory of morality, and being sensible good-hearted rogues they don't make a fuss. Yet all the time Defoe does think it wrong to steal or get into a fresh person's bed. (? thinks it wrong to be caught)

Moll's decency funnier than he intended? How just her reflections when she robs of its gold necklace the little girl returning from her dancing-class! No hypocrite. We laugh without bitterness or superiority. 'I spoke with a melancholy air, and said, "No, child; the boy is gone for a pint of ale for me"' seems consummate comedy, yet part of its effect accidental (she is about to steal a tankard). Intelligent cockney fun – cf. Reg. Palmer – with Sich is life for a philosophy, and Newgate in the place of Hell.

An untypical passage:

Let them say what they please of our sex not being able to keep a secret, my life is a plain conviction to me of the contrary; but be it our sex, or the man's sex, a secret of moment should always have a confidant, a bosom friend, to whom we may communicate the joy of it, or the grief of it, be it which it will, or it will be a double weight upon the spirits, and perhaps become even insupportable in itself; and this I appeal to all human testimony for the truth of.

And this is the cause why many times men as well as women, and men of the greatest and best qualities other ways, yet have found themselves weak in this part, and have not been able to bear the weight of a secret joy or of a secret sorrow, but have been obliged to disclose it, even for the mere giving vent to themselves, and to unbend the mind oppressed with the load and weights which attended it. Nor was this any token of folly or thoughtlessness at all, but a natural consequence of the thing; and such people, had they struggled longer with the oppression, would certainly have told it in their sleep . . .

Moll still speaks, but surely with Defoe's voice. As a rule he says 'Of course I believe in Infinity', like the bus-drivers when pressed – and there is no more to be said: it shuts the door more strongly than denial.

To cheat a man, and to tell him so pleasantly afterwards, at the right moment, is to slide further into his good graces. A pretentious psychologist would labour long ere he grasped this truth, but D. knows it straight away. What happened to him in Newgate? Was it the creative germ?

Form of the book springs out of the subject: Moll turns from husbands to shop-lifting as the years pass, then is punished and repents. Also a slight attempt to make her brother-husband the centre of a plot, but no emphasis falls here in the end; when she and her Lancashire husband encounter him, he is deprived of eyesight and intellect to save trouble, and the episode closes amid the commercial urbanities of her misbegotten son. The tradesman-husband, the legal one, contributes nothing after his disappearance. Evidently Defoe wrote ahead, leaving a thread here and there, such as a child, on the chance of requiring it after, but really carried through on his impulses.

Style:

... a gentleman on horseback, and a page with a feather in his hat upon another horse.

I could make but little of my trade, only at a little country opera-house made a shift to carry off a gold watch from a lady's side, who was not only intolerably merry, but, as I thought, a little fuddled, which made my work much easier.

I say, there was no room to question the truth of it; I knew his clothes, I knew his horse, and I knew his face.

... the dress was indeed exceedingly surprising, perfectly new, very agreeable, and wonderful rich.

(*Roxana*; is 'wonderful' intentional?) [2]

Living Character in a novel best discovered by negative tests. If it is always startling us into approval it is a proof that it dies between the sentences. If a character lives, much else is apt to follow: we are distracted from deadness else-where. All characters alive, up to the edge of the book? Possible? Desirable? Happens in *War and Peace*, but that has no edges. Many books they might split; so a novelist's sterility may serve him well as well as badly.

Axiom: novel must have either one living character or a perfect pattern: fails otherwise. (Though what about *Moby Dick*?)

2. [The adverbial use of 'wonderful' – as indeed of 'exceeding' and 'perfect' – was common in Defoe's day.]

Telling the Story: atavistic element; shock-headed public gaping round the camp-fire, and only kept awake by *suspense*.[3] If story is about living beings, well and good, but public seems equally thrilled by dummies, indeed prefers them because they recall the other stories that lie piled in its mind. ('Oh no, that won't do, it's what we should say ourselves,' they complained about *The Prisoners of War* at Woolaston.)

N.B.: story-teller needn't pick up loose threads. As long as he keeps his shock-heads excited he needs no plot. Films. Reading aloud – Scott said to seem better then.

Pattern or Rhythm seems to me the third great element in a novel, but these are words easier to use than to define. They have some connection with the Story (which must in its turn have some connection with living Character. The Pattern may be the Plot – in *The Brothers Karamazov* they run together so far as either is present: strengthens the book when this happens. Or they may run in different directions, as in *Bleak House*, where the plot is a complicated maze and of interest to detectives, and the pattern little more than the driftings of the London fog. (Mem.: read *The Golden Bowl*; one can approach the meaning of pattern by seeing what James sacrificed to attain it ... snipping beetroots and spring onions for his salad: for I know he would keep among the vegetables, if only because their reproductive organs are not prominent ...)

P. Lubbock's *Roman Pictures* has a competent machine-made pattern. He thinks (*The Craft of Fiction* – a sensitive yet poor-spirited book) that the aim of a novel should be capable of being put into a phrase, 'ten words that reveal its unity', and so boggles at *War and Peace*, though he 'duly'

3. Or by *surprise* and the hope of further surprises. But this assumes a subtler audience, and leads us nearer to literature.

recognizes its vitality. So Pattern or Rhythm shouldn't be difficult to define for him: for he connects them with the plot, and thinks that can be tersely stated. Must I read him through?

Immediate Past is like a stuffy room, and the succeeding generation waste their time in trying to tolerate it. All they can do is to go out leaving the door open behind them. The room may be spacious, witty, harmonious, friendly, but it smells, and there is no getting round this. Hence letters to *The Times* on the one hand and broken windows on the other. 'What a pity the young are not more tolerant!' Quite so. But what a pity there is such a thing as death, for that is the real difficulty. The apartments occupied by the succeeding generation will smell equally in their turn. (Writers whom I find smell: H. James, Meredith, Stevenson: and if Hardy doesn't it's not because his novels are better than the other three – they are not so good – but because of the injection into them of great poetry.)

Ladder of the shocked, starting from Adam. M. Arnold shocked people by *Empedocles on Etna* and was shocked in his old age by Mr H. A. Jones, who is now shocked by every-thing himself and whom I have difficulty in conceiving as a fresh young thing – easier to enter into the youth of M. A.[4] Thus the literature of the immediate past cannot free us from the tyranny of time. Its limitations evoke our own, date us, and we retort by accusing it of dating. Impossible to read a Meredith as simply and fairly as a Fielding, with one eye fixed on the author's interests and the other on his achievement. (Read *Tom Jones* and *Evan Harrington* when I had chickenpox, 19, and felt this strongly.)

4. [The manuscript here has the additional words 'who is now shocked', but these seem to represent no more than the literary equiva-lent of a gramophone record stuck in a groove.]

H.C.D.[5] Novels, *because they are written in prose*,[6] all make some pretence of representing ordinary life. This is their H.C.D. – low and uninteresting: but above it they begin to differentiate. Not a bad plan to think a novel's going to be a letter. Think of novelists all writing letters at once in a sort of B. M. Reading Room and getting books at the same time on various subjects.

Ordinary daily life is full of the time sense. 'She rang the bell and the footman answered it.' 'The general gave orders to cease firing.' 'H.R.H. pulled the string which released the Union Jack, and Mr Tweedie's monument was at once exposed to view.' We don't learn why the Prince was there or what the monument was like; to answer such questions requires other apparatus; but we do learn that one thing happens after another, and this obsession with the time-sequence fills our daily life and is the sorry common unit of the novel. (If the time-sequence is taken seriously it produces a sad effect – *Old Wives' Tale*[7] – but not a tragic one: *War and Peace* depends for its effect on something else. If taken either lightly or instinctively it leads to a slackening of emotion and a shallowness of judgement. Consequently many novelists have been inclined to play tricks with time. Proust, Emily Brontë, Sterne, Conrad all discovered that

5. [*Sic.* Forster presumably means either Highest Common Factor or Lowest Common Denominator – the former being perhaps more accurate, the latter more frequently used in metaphorical contexts.]

6. Then have they also the same H.C.D. as plays? Perhaps I am altogether on too vague a track, and this pretence of a time-sense may be common to the whole of literature and may be implied when one word is written after another. Yet it is *not* implied in music nor in words under their musical aspect: these have nothing to do with the time-sequence of ordinary life.

7. Which, like Couperus's *Old People and the Things that Pass*, fails of greatness because its main theme is 'People get old'. Of course they do. Daily life is the business of getting old – that is the time-sequence as it touches humanity and all creation. And a great book must rest on something more than an 'of course'.

he was not exactly their friend, or only friendly for moments, and that he must be kept in his place if they were to do what they wished.)

Robinson Crusoe an English book, and only the English could have accepted it as adult literature: comforted by feeling that the life of adventure could be led by a man duller than themselves. No gaiety, wit or invention. (Contrast Friday with Amy in *Roxana*; or the two storms.) Boy Scout manual. Unlike Moll or Roxana or Selkirk himself, Crusoe never develops or modifies.

As much bored as I was 30 years ago. Its only literary merit is the well-contrived crescendo of the savages. Historically important, no doubt, and the parent of other insincerities, such as *Treasure Island*. Nearly as bad as *Captain Singleton*, and I shan't read Part 2.

I took it by another handle, and asked him who made the sea, the ground we walked on, and the hills and woods? He told me it was one old Benamuckee, that lived beyond all: he could describe nothing of this great person, but that he was very old, much older, he said, than the sea or the land, than the moon or the stars. I asked him then, if this old person had made all things, why did not all things worship him? He looked very grave, and with a perfect look of innocence said, All things do say O to him. I asked him if the people who die in his country went away anywhere? He said, Yes; they all went to Benamuckee: then I asked him whether these they eat went thither too! He said, Yes.

Friday then 'listened with great attention, and received with pleasure the notion of Jesus Christ being sent to redeem us'. But without surprise. Defoe never really leaves Newgate or Bartholomew Close, though I must grant him an occasional triumph in the realm of the half-sincere. For the above passage is good though silly – how silly when we place it by

> his art is of such power,
> It would control my dam's god, Setebos.

Defoe never makes that accidental approach to science that is one of the achievements of poetry. Crusoe's island differs from Prospero's because there are no real savages in it, and not a glimmer of primitive religion, and this difference is connected with an imaginative gulf.

I intended to do a note on *Roxana* too. It's as good as *Moll*, but lacks the thieving, and consequently suffers in its form, and in its morality also, which becomes purely sexual and therefore dates. (By the way, why is D. only keen on the sexual life of women? His approach to men's – in *Colonel Jack* – is perfunctory. Only when there is a woman in the case does he warm up.) The raping of Amy and the storm going to Holland: best I ever read.

Virginia says: 3 cardinal points of perspective, God, man, Nature, and Crusoe snubs us on each and forces us to contemplate 'a large earthenware pot' – i.e. Defoe has a sense of reality which she also calls 'common sense'. Passing on to the dreary Bloomsbury conclusion that the pot's perspective may be as satisfying as the universe if the writer believes in a pot with sufficient intensity. I say such a writer's a bore merely.

Gulliver is Robinson Crusoe in Fairy Land. People are smaller than he is, or larger, or horses, and he works out the consequences. He has a bad temper in the place of R.'s none, and moral indignation pushes him towards fantasy in Laputa, the most successful of his voyages. Inferior to *Erewhon* and even to the *Memoirs of a Midget*, because he never succeeds in making the reader think that he deals with living stuff. Indignation isn't a creative force: 'Come, you're cross, and what for?' we exclaim.

The book is illustrated with maps. Did Swift compose these? They are not inspiring.

[*Apropos* Laputa:] 'He said they [the *Struldbruggs*] commonly acted like Mortals, till about Thirty Years old,

after which by Degrees they grew melancholy and dejected'
etc. – but I will transcribe this passage into my anthology,
under Old Age: here observing that it is Swift at his best.

Perhaps too there is a sort of dried poetry in these
18th-century writers which is nearer the true thing than the
upholstery of Scott. If steeped in the right liquid Crusoe and
Gulliver and Tristram might expand – they wouldn't rot.
But the Romantics thought it was the right thing to be
poetical. They wouldn't tolerate us.

Dates of 18th-century novels:

> 1722   *Moll Flanders*
> 1726   *Gulliver*

and a gap of about 20 years before Richardson, Fielding and
Smollett all get going together, while Sterne and Goldsmith
start off in the 60s.

Border Cases: are these novels – *Pilgrim's Progress, Marius
the Epicurean, The Bible in Spain, The Adventures of a Younger
Son, A Journal of the Plague Year, Zuleika Dobson, Rasselas,
Green Mansions*? And if we answer this question do we
appreciate them better or not so well?

I can reply to neither, nor to that other question of subject versus treatment, and my temperament is to dismiss all
this sort of stuff as the product of the examination-system,
or as the need of talking seriously which people seem to experience after they reach a certain age. The desire to appear
weighty often disguises itself as disinterested curiosity.

Clarissa Harlowe. Have read 1/3 of. Long books, when
read, are usually overpraised, because the reader wishes to
convince others and himself that he has not wasted his time.
Cf. St Paul's argument for immortality. Certainly I am
bored, but the book is not tedious through repetition – the
endless variants and modulations are not in themselves

interesting enough – it's that. I never mock. Granted her premises about copulation and relations, Clarissa deduces with delicacy and truth. Within her conventions, she is sound. She is tragic and charming. Richardson had a tragic mind. [*The passage quoted on pp. 31-2*] cannot come out of shallowness. Cf. Kath. of Arr. [i.e. Katherine of Aragon in *Henry VIII*].

The book raises the question of subject-matter. Within its limits it's great. But what limits!

Provincialism. We must remember the mountains that lie outside our territory, but not below our horizon – Tolstoy, Dostoyevsky, Proust. They will give scale to our criticism and stop us from being too grave over *The Heart of Midlothian* or pottering too long over *Cranford*. The great English novelists – Defoe, Richardson, Sterne, Dickens, Jane Austen, E. Brontë – are either not great enough, or perhaps not of the particular greatness that keeps the small fry in awe. Which is well enough for literature but harmful for criticism. English poetry excels in quality as well as quantity. English fiction, though profuse, does not contain the best stuff yet written, either in vitality or intensity.

To take the reader into your confidence about your *characters*: always means intellectual and emotional lowering. You try to cover up your deficiencies as a creator by turning friendly. Like standing a man a drink that he may not criticize your opinions. Provincial chattiness. Fielding and Thackeray. Scott when he tries it is awful. Always leads to facetiousness and an invitation to see how the figures hook up behind. 'Doesn't A look nice?' 'Let's think why B does that.' 'C always was a mystery.' Intimacy is gained at the cost of illusion and of nobility. Nothing has dragged the novel down more (though what about *Tristram Shandy*?).

Confidences about the *universe* are a less serious matter.

Does it hurt the characters if the novelist steps outside them and generalizes as to the conditions under which life, he thinks, is carried on? Tolstoy, Hardy, Conrad.

[*Apropos 'characters', above*:] Now, what about intermittent knowledge? The average novelist is omniscient when it suits his book, then shamelessly draws a curtain and shakes his head. Condemned by purists. I see no objection if he bounces the reader successfully. Far less fatal than chatting. Indeed this ability to expand or contract perception without being detected is one of the advantages of the novel form, and has a parallel in our perception of life: we are stupider at some times than at others, and this intermittence lends variety and colour to the experiences we receive. Nothing to make a fuss over here.

All the same this important subject must be pursued, the academic divisions examined – cf. 'The Fiction Factory' in my scrapbook, p. 84 [*i.e. Appendix B*] – and the more general question is raised: why is it right to deceive the readers in some ways and wrong in others?

The Ambassadors (analysed in *Craft of Fiction*, [pp. 156–71]). Pattern exquisitely woven. Strether and Chad change places like Paphnuce and Thaïs in A. France, but with qualifications. S., sent to rescue C. to *commonplace and commerce* [*sic*][8] from going to the bad in Paris, finds that C. hasn't gone to the bad, but has been redeemed and enlarged by Mme de Vionnet: he gives up his mission and hope of marrying Mrs Newsome, he fights for *Paris*[9] instead

8. ['Footnote' consisting of parts of the passage quoted on pp. 139–40, followed by the comment:] Typical example of H. J.'s power of indicating instantaneously and constantly that a character is second-rate, deficient in sensitiveness, abounding in the wrong sort of worldliness. The vitality with which he endows such a character always increases its absurdity.

9. ['Footnote' consisting of the passage quoted on pp. 138–9.]

of against it. Then, out in the country, he encounters C. and Mme de V. out on the spree – and that they should be ashamed of it and tell him lies shows him that they are *vulgar*[10] and that the force of his imagination has more spiritual value than their youth. C. will tire of her, he will go back to America. S. will have lost – and gained – everything.

Pattern woven – at what sacrifice? Most of human life has to disappear – all fun, all rapid motion, carnality, etc., and 9/10 of heroism. Maimed creatures can alone breathe in his pages – maimed yet specialized: cf. the exquisite deformities that appear in Egyptian art under Akhnaton – all heads and no legs, but nevertheless charming. Is this maiming of the human worth while except in the interests of the superhuman? The curtailment and specialization of our fabric with H. J. doesn't give a religion or a philosophy, only a pattern into which cocktails and stands won't fit. When his characters say to each other 'But you're wonderful', 'But you're magnificent' they are right in the first case, wrong in the second. H. J. very intelligent, self-denial and timidity with him almost the same thing. His art so sure and dominating that it pacifies us while we read. But it doesn't satisfy us. We still say 'This won't do' and still he replies 'Perhaps not, but it does for my poor book.'

Style. However hard you shake his sentences, no banality falls out. But he is rather apt to have a good sentence, and round it, like suckers, others that are less good and connected with their parent by verbal misunderstandings.

Characters. Main one usually an observer who tries to influence the action and who through his failure to do so gains extra opportunities for observation (Strether, Fleda in *The Spoils of Poynton*). Often has a mother in a [*sic*] back-

10. ['Footnote' consisting of the greater part of the passage quoted on p. 141.]

ground and a *nameless*[11] disease. Then the vulgar comics as above (Henrietta Stackpole an early example). And other characters such as such an observer can observe through lens procured from first-class oculist. Introduce Emma or Tom Jones into an H.J., they would become not unsuitable but invisible.

Round versus Flat characters – types, humours. One of my lectures on People will turn on this distinction. Tolstoy *the* rounder. And *Jane Austen* – infelicitously described as a miniaturist on ivory. Carves cherry stones if you like. But even Miss Bates has a mind, even Elizabeth Elliot a heart. Discovery that Lady Bertram has a moral outlook shocked me at first. I had not realized the solidity of an art which kept such an aspect in reserve, and placed her always on a sofa with pug.

Dickens's characters are types, but his vitality causes them to vibrate a little, so that they borrow his life and appear to live their own. Mr Micawber, Pickwick, Mrs Jellaby, live, but not in the sense that we can turn them round and see new aspects. Contrast Pickwick with Falstaff. *Wells* – like Dickens – doesn't really create: Kipps and the aunt in *Tono-Bungay* the chief exceptions. Author's vitality again.

Parallels between *Dickens and Wells*: low birth, cockney outlook, comedy, social problems – relish indignation. Put people into their books and deny they have done so afterwards. W.'s power of observation stronger – he photographs those he meets and agitates the photographs. D. relies more on types.

11. N.B. How he hates naming anything! Contrast the anonymous article manufactured by the Newsomes with *Tono-Bungay*; cf. *The Pattern on* [*i.e. Figure in*] *the Carpet*; and listen to the uncomfortable words of H.G.W. himself: 'James demands homogeneity. Why should a book have that? For a picture it's reasonable, because you have to see it all at once . . .'[*Then as on p. 144.*] – *Boon*, pp. 102–6. And to H. J.'s reply: [*lacuna*].

Flat character can always be recognized by the reader whenever it reappears. Hence its advantage for story-telling. And authors who do work in the round, like Proust with M. de Charlus, often have their minor characters flat – Comtesse Molé. Useful in social pictures. It is incidentally condemned by *Norman Douglas*:

I spoke just now of the novelist's touch in biography. What is this touch? [*Then as on p. 75.*]

– *A Plea for Better Manners* (attack on D. H. Lawrence).

N.B. Modern tendency to *pseudo-roundness*. Something contradictory or incredible is said towards the end of a book about a flat character, in order to persuade the reader of its profundity and rebuke the shallowness of his previous judgements.

Evil. Feebly envisaged in English fiction, which seldom soars below misconduct or evades the clouds of mysteriousness. *Either* sexual and social: *or* a special style, with implications of poetry, is thought necessary when describing it. I don't believe evil exists: but most writers think it *ought* to exist and form the backside of their plots: and one or two think it does exist. Dostoyevsky. *Melville*:

This great power of blackness in him [Hawthorne][12] derives its force from its appeals to that Calvinistic sense of Innate Depravity and Original Sin, from whose visitations, in some shape or other, no deeply thinking mind is always and wholly free. For, in certain moods, no man can weigh this world without throwing in something, somehow like Original Sin, to strike the uneven balance.

This is playing the clean game as against the muddled or moral ones which were all that Hawthorne (as a matter of fact) knew.

Billy Budd has goodness – faint beside Alyosha's and

12. [Forster's interpolation.]

rather alloyed by H.M.'s suppressed homosex: still he has goodness of the glowing aggressive sort which cannot exist unless it has evil to consume: goodness

[*the first passage quoted on p. 129*]

Speaking of Claggart, whom Billy kills:

Civilization, especially if of the austerer sort, is auspicious to it [i.e. to Natural Depravity].[13] It . . . has [*then as on p. 129*].

Don't know what H.M. means, but he knows, and what grand conception of characters are [*sic*] consequently possible for him.

Moby Dick also a struggle, and of course a bigger one than Billy Budd's, but Ahab and the whale – what do they stand for? 'Oh, what quenchless feud is this, that Time hath with the sons of Men' (*Pierre*) and perhaps that is all.

Other claimants to Satanic intimacy: the Pan school, petering out in Hichens and E. F. Benson – Hawthorne's *Marble Faun* an early specimen of it – and Forrest Reid. Conrad? – scarcely claims. H.J. in *The Turn of the Screw* is merely declining to think about homosex, and the knowledge that he is declining throws him into the necessary fluster. Only a writer who has the sense of evil can make goodness readable. I come back to Melville and Dostoyevsky. Villains I haven't the spirits to give a separate note to, though they could form the basis of a long literary chat. Richardson, Dickens; influence of Germany; on and on.

Melville's apprehensions free from that personal worry that contracts Hawthorne or 'Mark Rutherford'. We are bigger, not smaller, after sharing them.

Boredom, avoidance of by modern writers, leads them into flimsiness. Bunny Garnett, though he has central conception, works thinking of the surface. A point of honour not

13. [Forster's interpolation.]

to be a bore. Boredom less prevalent in the age of faith. Dickens so far modern that he's only a bore when he is bad. But C. Brontë and G. Eliot positively progress while they massacre us.

Psychology of boredom? Ask Heard.

Bores and romanticism – not 18th century.

Great Expectations. Alliance between atmosphere and plot (the convicts) make [*sic*] it more solid and satisfactory than anything else of D. known to me. Very fine writing occasionally – end of Part 1:

> I walked away at a good pace, thinking it was easier to go than I had supposed it would be, and reflecting that it would never have done to have an old shoe thrown after the coach, in sight of all the High-street. I whistled and made nothing of going. But the village was very peaceful and quiet, and the light mists were solemnly rising, as if to show me the world, and I had been so innocent and little there, and all beyond was so unknown and great, that in a moment with a strong heave and sob I broke into tears. It was by the finger-post at the end of the village, and I laid my hand upon it, and said, 'Good-bye, O my dear, dear friend!'
> . . .
> We changed again, and yet again, and it was now too late and too far to go back, and I went on. And the mists had all solemnly risen now, and the world lay spread before me.

> THIS IS THE END OF THE FIRST STAGE OF
> PIP'S EXPECTATIONS

Pip adequate, Joe Gargery not a stick. Occasional hints not developed – e.g. Mrs G.'s (and Jagger's) character *does* nothing, Herbert Pocket's has to be revised. But all the defects are trivial, and the course of events is both natural and exciting. Now and then (e.g. in the return of Magwitch) D. grasps at subtleties which would impede him if he grasped them always. Pip's cold disgust and fundamental decency. Beating heart instead of good digestion of Scott.

Chilly mist – chill without mist in *D. Copperfield*. Autumnal England. And the river – cf. *Our Mutual Friend*.

Cannot express its merits properly. One of the few master-pieces in my copious catalogue.

Worse at the end. Nearly all novels go off at the end. Exceptions: the artists – Jane Austen, Richardson, Henry James, D. Garnett; the fantasists – Sterne. 'Nor can I go on, without a reflection on those accidental meetings which, though they happen every day, seldom excite our surprise but upon some extraordinary occasion.' – *Vicar of Wakefield*. Nor could he indeed. Pity there isn't another convention, which allows a novelist to stop when he's getting out of his depth. V. of W. gets out of his half way through – after the painting of the family group with Mrs Primrose as Venus all the grace and wit vanishes. Olivia's elopement breaks the comedy, and the happy ending to the tragedy makes all worse than ever – cf. *Lolly Willowes* too – how silly the book becomes when the witchcraft starts, how worse than silly when it culminates.

Bunny's books are so good because they *don't* go off. *A Man at the Zoo* fails at the end because the author doesn't put the lady into the cage as well as the man. But [*Lady into*] *Fox* and *Sailor* [*i.e. The Sailor's Return*] strengthen steadily.

Time bears all its sons away unless they look sharp. Something numbing in the numbing sequence of birth, days, nights, death, and consequently something unsatisfactory in a *story*, which is essentially a narrative in time, tempered by reminiscences and prophecies, and must be either insincere or depressing. A story is the basis of all novels but it can't alone form a great book, because it is tethered to time. Supposed the healthiest form of art, its real moral is decay, and various *escapes* are attempted besides the insincere 'they all lived happily ever after' and the sincere but terrible grasping of the river of Time by the horns (*Old Wives' Tale*).

Interest the reader in *people*[14] – not in what happens next. Or in the scenes through which the people pass. Or get an emphasis other than the time one – *plot or pattern*[15] (have not worked this out yet: arrival of art). Or reveal or imply incidentally something that transcends – *Moby Dick*. Or play about – Sterne, Peacock, de la Mare, N. Douglas.

Human Nature less mysterious than it was to anyone who has the inclination to observe it. We know fairly well now – not *what* people are going to do but why they have done it. Man's destiny will always be an object for speculation, but his nature (like his origin) is getting pinned down (e.g. Denis Mansfield's conceit is clearly not an extra defect but an attempt to conceal his imbecility).

Does it develop – except by its power of observing itself?

Aims and Achievements. The scientist aims at truth, and succeeds if he finds it. The artist aims at truth and succeeds if he raises the emotions. The orator aims at raising the emotions and succeeds if he raises them. This is true even of books that are planned beforehand: writer may hope that fire will descend on his skeleton, yet his concern is anatomy, not the striking of a match. Still truer of books that are not planned beforehand, but grow.

From which spring 2 questions:

(1) Bad aims – i.e. to make money or give pain to living people or to deceive: only a moralist can assert these always lead to bad results. Defoe's novels are morally on the level of Opal Whiteley or the *Diary of a Young Lady of Fashion* –

14. Seems obvious, yet as soon as we have admitted the importance of people we have struck a blow at story-telling pure and simple. 'A story is a narrative in time about ninepins' is an easier thesis than 'A story is a narrative in time about people', because people are so arresting that they can survive their own decay.

15. Say – plot intellectual, pattern aesthetic, you have to think out the peripeteia of *Bleak House*, but must have taste to appreciate that of *Thaïs* or *Together*.

designed to take in the ill-informed, for money. Trollope wrote for money – [*lacuna*] words before breakfast. *Joseph Andrews* caricatures. Wells in *New Machiavelli*, etc.

(2) Have forgotten what it was to be.

'**Her Business** is not half so much with the human heart as with the human eyes, mouth, hands, and feet. What sees keenly, speaks aptly, moves flexibly, it suits her to study; but what throbs fast and full, though hidden, what the blood rushes through, what is the unseen seat of life and the sentient target of death – this **Miss Austen** ignores.' Charlotte Brontë, quoted by H. Read.

Aristotle versus Alain on Character, etc.

All human happiness or misery takes the form of action; the end for which we live is a certain kind of activity, not a quality. Character gives us qualities, but it is in our actions – what we do – that we are happy or the reverse. In a play accordingly they do not act in order to portray the Characters; they include the Characters for the sake of the action . . .

Four points to aim at in a character (in Tragedy): good – appropriate – real, which is not the same as good and appropriate in our sense of the term – and consistent; if inconsistent, consistently so. [*This page of the Commonplace Book has been divided into two columns, and the above entry (except for the heading) written in the left-hand column. The quotation from Aristotle was presumably to have been matched by one from Alain.*]

Preceding 16 pages[16] all refer to my own course *Aspects of the Novel*. Housman came to two and I called on him on the strength of this, but he took no notice.

16. [In point of fact, pp. 20–35 (except for one extraneous entry, omitted here) and the first entry on p. 36, opposite which, in the left-hand margin of p. 37, this note is written. A further entry on p. 36 has no apparent connection with *Aspects of the Novel*.]

APPENDIX B

THE FICTION FACTORY

Forster's review (Daily News, *23 April 1919; signed 'by a novelist') of* Materials and Methods of Fiction *by Clayton Hamilton (see pages 29–30; see also Appendix C).*

THE poor dear novel! The poor, poor little thing! Who would have thought that a Mr Clayton Hamilton, instigated by Mr Brander Matthews, had been scanning it narrowly from on high! It ran about so happily, like an inoffensive hen, and scratching in the dust and the grass of life it routed out so many objects, some valuable, some not. And lo! suddenly down swoops the American eagle! Not that the eagle is the least unkind or rough. He merely lays the hen on her back and tells her what she has been doing. And if she squawks faintly that she didn't know she was doing anything particular at all, the eagle screams his acquiescence, and notes, for the benefit of future hens, the importance of the subconscious element in fictional art. Here it all is. A revised and enlarged edition, too. Here is the 'necessary triple process' through which every novelist must pass (namely, scientific discovery, philosophic understanding, and artistic expression). Here are the three merits he must aim at (namely, momentous material, masterly method, and important personality). Here are the nine ways in which he may make use of the weather. 'Although the weather,' we are told, 'is a subject upon everybody's tongue, there are very few people who are capable of talking about it with intelligence and art.' When they write novels their incapacity is further illustrated. Let them, therefore, study the weather in theory and practice, at the same time memorizing the following rules and examples.

For the weather may be, firstly, 'non-existent, as in a nursery tale'. Then it may be 'decorative' (Pierre Loti). 'Utilitarian' (*The Mill on the Floss*). 'Illustrative' (*The Egoist*). 'Planned in pre-established harmony' (Fiona Macleod). 'In emotional contrast' (*The Master of Ballantrae*). 'Determinative of action' (in a Kipling story a man proposes to the wrong girl, owing to a sandstorm). 'A controlling influence' (*Richard Feverel*). And, ninthly, it may be itself a hero (Vesuvius in *The Last Days of Pompeii*). The hen rises. Now she is wise. But I do not think she will ever feel up to laying an egg again.

The truth is that good writing can only be learned from good writing. Mr Hamilton glibly agrees, and at the end of each chapter he says: 'Suggested Reading. Read the most important works of fiction mentioned in this chapter.' But what he doesn't see (at least, he doesn't put it in this edition, though he may tabulate it in the next) is that we learn not from studying a book, but from enjoying it, and that in consequence there is nothing to be learned from his. He has read widely and he is clear and he is catholic, desolatingly catholic, but he has neither emotion nor taste, and so cannot provoke those qualities in others. 'Of course not. They are innate,' he smiles. Of course. But his book denies this truth in spirit, though it may affirm it in words, and if it fell into the hands of a young writer would certainly do him harm rather than good, and lead him to believe that fiction can be manufactured by attention to externals. A machine-made article may be better or worse made, but it remains a machine-made article, and however tippy the processes it can never have individual distinction. It may have the coherence of logic, it will never have the coherence of life. 'La vérité en toute chose étant extrêmement délicate et fugitive ce n'est pas à la dialectique qu'il est donné de l'atteindre,' says Renan, and no amount of tabulating and conscientious reading can help a writer who would be creative, while the writer who is not creative will be helped by them only too much. Never again, for instance, will he get muddled over the Point of View. For it may be:

Class I: External
    (i)   Point of View of Leading Actor
    (ii)   Of subsidiary Actor
    (iii)   Of different Actors
    (iv)   Epistolary
Class II: Internal
    (i)   Omniscient
    (ii)   Limited
    (iii)   Rigidly restricted

He will be enabled, with fatal ease, to turn out seven different kinds of novels, and if in each he adopts a different attitude towards the weather he will total sixty-three. Oh yes, and there are two 'tones', Impersonal and Personal. A hundred and twenty-six. But I retire from the roar and the clanking. The poor dear novel! The poor, poor little thing!

APPENDIX C

MATERIALS AND METHODS
OF FICTION

Some passages in Clayton Hamilton's book referred to by Forster (pp. 29–30 and Appendix B). Note that the 'Suggested Reading' exhortation quoted by Forster occurs only once; and that in the 'Point of View' schema Forster has reversed 'External' and 'Internal'. Page numbers are those of the 1918 edition reviewed by Forster.

Uses of the Weather – All that has been said thus far of setting in general applies of course to one of the most interesting of its elements – the weather. In simple stories like the usual nursery tale, the weather may be non-existent. Or it may exist mainly for a decorative purpose, like the frequent golden oriental dawns of Spenser's poem or the superb and colourful symphonies of sky and sea in Pierre Loti's *Iceland Fisherman*. It may be used as a utilitarian adjunct to the action: at the end of *The Mill on the Floss*, as we have already noted, the rains descend and the flood comes merely for the purpose of drowning Tom and Maggie. Or it may be employed to illustrate a character: we are told of Clara Middleton, in *The Egoist*, that she possesses the 'art of dressing to suit the season and the sky'; and therefore the look of the atmosphere at any hour helps to convey to us a sense of her appearance. Somewhat more artistically, the weather may be planned in pre-established harmony with the mood of the characters: this expedient is wonderfully used in the wild and wind-swept tales of Fiona Macleod. On the other hand, the weather may stand in emotional contrast with the characters: the Master of

179

ASPECTS OF THE NOVEL

Ballantrae and Mr Henry fight their duel on a night of absolute stillness and stifling cold. Again, the weather may be used to determine the action: in Mr Kipling's early story called 'False Dawn', the blinding sandstorm causes Saumarez to propose to the wrong girl. Or it may be employed as a controlling influence over character: the tremendous storm towards the end of *Richard Feverel*, in the chapter entitled 'Nature Speaks', determines the return of the hero to his wife. In some cases, even, the weather itself may be the real hero of the narrative: the great eruption of Vesuvius in *The Last Days of Pompeii* dominates the termination of the story.

Although the weather is a subject upon everybody's tongue, there are very few people who are capable of talking about it with intelligence and art. Very few writers of fiction – and nearly all of them are recent – have exhibited a mastery of the weather, – a mastery based at once upon a detailed and accurate observation of natural phenomena and a philosophic sense of the relation between these phenomena and the concerns of human beings. Perhaps in no other detail of craftsmanship does Robert Louis Stevenson so clearly prove his mastery as in his marshalling of the weather, always vividly and truthfully described, to serve a purpose always fitting to his fictions. [pp. 112–14]

Two Tones of Narrative, Impersonal and Personal:

1. *The Impersonal Tone.* In employing every phase of the external point of view except the one which has been last discussed, the author is free to choose between two very different tones of narrative – the impersonal and the personal. He may either obliterate or emphasize his own personality as a factor in the story. The great epics and folk-tales have all been told impersonally ... Many modern authors, like Sir Walter Scott, instinctively assume the epic attitude toward their characters and incidents: they look

upon them with a large unconsciousness of self and depict
them just as anyone would see them. Other authors, like
Mr William Dean Howells, strive deliberately to keep the
personal note out of their stories: self-consciously they
triumph over self in the endeavour to leave their characters
alone.

2. *The Personal Tone.* But novelists of another class prefer
to admit frankly to the reader that the narrator who stands
apart from all the characters and writes about them in the
third person is the author himself. They give a personal
tone to the narrative; they assert their own peculiarities of
taste and judgement, and never let you forget that they,
and they alone, are telling the story. The reader has to see
it through their eyes. It is in this way, for example, that
Thackeray displays his stories – pitying his characters, admiring them, making fun of them, or loving them, and
never letting slip an opportunity to chat about the matter
with his readers ... It is true, of course, that the strictest
artists in fiction, like Guy de Maupassant, prefer to tell their
tales impersonally: they leave their characters rigidly alone,
and allow the reader to see them without looking through
the author's personality. But there is a type of literature
wherein the chief charm for the reader lies in the fact that
he is permitted to see things through the author's mind ...
The merit, or the defect, of the method in any case is a
question not of rules and regulations but of the tone and
quality of the author's mind. Whether or not he may safely
obtrude himself into his fictions depends entirely on who he
is. This is a matter more of personality than of art: and
what might be insufferable with one author may stand as
the main merit of another. [pp. 133–5]

APPENDIX D

THE ART OF FICTION

Broadcast talk, B.B.C. Eastern Service, 24 November 1944; from a typescript in the B.B.C. archives. The text given here incorporates manuscript changes (some in Forster's hand, others probably made with his approval by his producer), and omits some concluding and recapitulatory remarks which have been deleted, apparently by Forster.

THE art of fiction. The art of the novel. Yes, but which novel? I have jotted down the names of half a dozen novels for us to think about. Here is the list: *Tristram Shandy* by Sterne; *Emma* by Jane Austen; *Moby Dick* by Herman Melville; *Bleak House* by Dickens; *The Ambassadors* by Henry James; and D. H. Lawrence's *The White Peacock*. Here are six good novels. What shall we say about their art? I'll repeat the names. *Tristram Shandy* – that's an eighteenth-century fantasy where the hero never gets born. *Emma* – here everything is reasonable and regular, the characters function, the action proceeds, the atmosphere is lively yet temperate, the outcome is high domestic comedy. *Moby Dick* – *Moby Dick* is very different, partly because the hero is a whale: it's a yarn about the sea, but it is also a meditation on the mystery of evil, which the whale embodies. *Bleak House* – that is a warm-hearted story about human beings, dozens of them, in an immensely complicated plot, mixed up with a criticism of the Law's Delays. *The Ambassadors* – in this novel Henry James analyses the development of a sensitive American who is dispatched to Paris to rescue one of his compatriots from its temptations, and who himself gets involved in Paris, city of light and beauty. And *The White*

Peacock – it is a masterpiece of immaturity, colours, flowers, the menace and enchantment of sex, recorded anyhow by an inspired child. All these six novels are good, and so we ought to be able to deduce from them what the art of fiction is.

We ought to, but can we? The novel is a literary form so wide in its range that generalizations about it are almost impossible. It's much more difficult to pin down the novel to its job than – say, the play, or the lyric poem, or even the short story. The play – that's going to be acted, so certain conventions are imposed on it by the stage and by the presence of an audience. The lyric poem – that is of the nature of a song, and it will tend to express one main emotion. The short story – that has the same medium as the novel, but it is short, and so it must calculate beforehand what effect it wants to produce, and produce it or fail. The novel, in my view, has not any rules, and so there is no such thing as the art of fiction. There's only the particular art that each novelist employs in the execution of his particular book. The art Sterne employs in writing *Tristram Shandy* is contrary to the art of Jane Austen in *Emma*. Sterne wants to be episodic and fantastic and to tease us with tricks. Jane Austen, in the quiet chosen area of Highbury, wants to work out a domestic comedy. If either of these great writers tried to borrow the art of the other, their work would fly to pieces at once. They have a common medium – prose – a common material – fiction – and their common aim: to do their job as well as possible.

Now books on the art of fiction have been written, some of them very good ones, and they have laid down rules which the novel ought to follow. It should be about human beings, they say, it should contain a narrative and some sort of plot, and it should be written from a definite point of view. This doctrine of 'the point of view' is a most interesting one, and I'll be coming back to it. Let's go back now to the six novels on our list, and put them through some tests. *Tristram Shandy* – that's about human beings, but they are presented very oddly; there is no plot or story in the ordinary sense, and the main interest is the fantastic happenings, and the obstinacy of inanimate objects, like Dr Slop's bag, which seems almost alive. If you lay down rules for the novel, and then apply them to *Tristram Shandy*, you have to admit that it wasn't a novel. You have been enjoying it – but it wasn't a novel. Pass on to Jane Austen's *Emma*. *Emma* does fulfil the tests. It is about human beings, it contains a story and a plot, and it is related from one point of view, namely the heroine's. Miss Austen tells us all about Emma, and we see the action and the other characters through Emma's eyes. Our spirits rise: our rules are working and here's a novel which really is a novel. Our spirits fall when we come to *Moby Dick*. In *Moby Dick*, though we have human beings and adventure, the main interest is the metaphysical problem of evil, and evil is embodied in Moby Dick – a white whale, whose pursuit and death involves the universe. Although *Moby Dick* is as far removed from *Tristram Shandy* as pole from pole, yet they have something in common which is absent from *Emma*: the element of the non-human. When that element is frivolous, as in *Tristram Shandy*, 'fantasy' is a good name for it. When it is serious, as in *Moby Dick*, we call it mystic or cosmic. After reading *Moby Dick* you will have enhanced your sense of wonder, you will have increased the size of your universe, but you will have to dismiss it as not really a novel, because it hasn't kept to the rules.

Pass on to *Bleak House*. Is *Bleak House* really a novel? Almost – it is full of interesting human beings and has an enthralling plot. But it has a purpose – it denounces a social injustice, and ought a novel to do that? Ought it to usurp the function of a pamphlet? Moreover, it has not got a consistent point of view, as *Emma* had. Think of the first three chapters of *Bleak House*. In the opening chapter we see everything through Charles Dickens's eyes. He takes us into the Court of Chancery and explains all the people there. In the second chapter we still use Dickens's eyes, but for some unknown reason they begin to go weak: he can explain some of the characters to us – but not all. In the third chapter he adopts a totally different method, drops the omniscient, and inhabits a young lady, Esther Summerson, and we see everything through Esther's eyes, and nobody else's. Judged by the standards of the art of fiction – if there is an art – *Bleak House* is all to bits. Let us pass on to the *The Ambassadors*, by Henry James. Here all the rules are working nicely – even better than they did in Jane Austen. It is a story about human beings, their interests dominate, no metaphysical or social evils are stressed, there is development and dénouement, and the story is told consistently from one point of view – the viewpoint of the sensitive American, who comes to rescue a compatriot from the snares of nineteenth-century Paris, and becomes himself involved in those snares, but not in the same sense, for he grows to realize that Paris, unlike America, means civilization. *The Ambassadors* is a novel which fulfils all the rules of the novelist's art, if rules there be. Let us pass on to *The White Peacock*, by D. H. Lawrence. Here the rules won't work. We are scarcely in a story at all. We are in a poem, in a field of flowers that is being mown, in a wood by night, in the throes of adolescence, streaked by cruelty. *The White Peacock* is a book which it is easy to criticize and impossible to forget. It has taken us – goodness knows how – to a land of romance and disquiet which we should otherwise have missed.

So that's how the rules work, and you can adopt them or not as you like. You can either say that there is an art of fiction, and that *Emma* and *The Ambassadors* are perfect novels, that *Bleak House* is an imperfect one, and that

Tristram Shandy, *Moby Dick* and *The White Peacock* aren't
novels at all, much as you have enjoyed them. Or you can
say with me that there aren't any rules, that there is no art
of the novel, only the art which a writer requires for the
particular work he is engaged on. In my judgement,
Laurence Sterne, Jane Austen, Herman Melville, Charles
Dickens, Henry James, D. H. Lawrence, all employed the
art which was appropriate to their special problem and
their temperament, and I should say that the six books on
our list are six good novels and leave it like that.

But let's go a little further into the theory of the 'point of
view', for even if we don't accept it we shall be stimulated.
I am going to quote an admirable critic, Percy Lubbock,
who believes in the 'point of view', and discussed it in an
interesting book, *The Craft of Fiction*. 'The whole intricate
question of method, in the craft of fiction,' says Mr Lubbock,
'I take to be governed by the question of the point of view
– the question of the relation in which the narrator stands
to the story.' The novelist, he goes on, can either describe
the characters from outside, as an impartial or partial onlooker; or can assume omniscience, and describe them from
within; or he can place himself in the position of one of
them and affect to be in the dark as to the motives of the
rest. What he must not do is mix his methods, and change
from one point of view to another – as Dickens does in
Bleak House; he'll weaken the book; and Lubbock instances
Tolstoy's *War and Peace* as a novel which would have been
even greater if Tolstoy's viewpoint had been consistent. I
don't agree. I believe that a novelist can shift his viewpoint
if it comes off, and it came off with Dickens and Tolstoy.
Indeed, this power to expand and contract perception (of
which the shifting viewpoint is a symptom), this right to
intermittent knowledge – I find it one of the great advantages of the novel-form, and it has a parallel in our perception of life. We are stupider at some times than others,

aren't we: we can enter into other people's minds occasionally, but not always, because our own minds get tired, and this intermittence lends in the long run variety and colour to the experiences we receive. A number of novelists have behaved like this to the characters in their books, played fast and loose with them as it were, and I can't see why they should be blamed for doing this.

So next time you read a novel do look out for the 'point of view' – that is to say, the relation of the narrator to the story. Is he telling the story and describing the characters from the outside, or does he identify himself with one of the characters? Does he pretend that he knows and foresees everything? Or does he go in for being surprised? Does he shift his point of view – like Dickens in the first three chapters of *Bleak House*? And, if he does, do you mind? I don't.

ANNOTATED INDEX

SINCE the original 'index of main references' looks like Forster's own handiwork, I have made a point of ensuring that what Forster regarded as important is readily accessible, one way or another. Thus the heading 'pseudo-scholarship' has been preserved, 'novelist's touch, the' is recognizable as a subheading under 'novelist, the', and cross-references have been provided from 'flat characters' and 'round characters' to 'characters', where 'flat' and 'round' occur as subheadings.

The present much fuller index is intended to serve three purposes. Briefly, these are (1) the tracing of any given passage or *obiter dictum*, however imperfectly remembered; (2) the pinpointing of what Forster has said on any given topic; (3) the provision, in an unobtrusive yet accessible form, of brief expository notes. The index covers the appendices as well as the main text, with some resultant duplication and near-duplication: a page number between 155 and 175 (Appendix A, extracts from Forster's Commonplace Book) will often be found to indicate a passage or phrase very similar to an earlier passage or phrase indexed under the same heading or subheading. I hope that the facilitation of comparison between Forster's first and final thoughts will outweigh any annoyance suffered by readers indifferent to such details.

Heavily subdivided headings are of two kinds: major topics ('characters', 'story' etc.) and major novelists (Jane Austen, Dickens etc.). The two kinds are treated somewhat differently. Entries under major topics are arranged as follows: (*a*) main relevant passages, followed by (*b*) selected specific themes and phrases, in order of first page number; between these categories there is some overlap. Entries under major novelists are arranged as follows: (*a*) passages and remarks unsuitable for summarizing; (*b*) selected specific themes and phrases; (*c*) in some cases, quoted comments of other critics; and (*d*) references to individual works. These four categories, of which (*c*) and (*d*) are arranged alphabetically, are mutually exclusive, although two or more may be represented on any one page; thus where Forster, during an analysis of *The Antiquary* (pp. 45–50), makes a passing remark about Scott in general (p. 46), the analysis is indexed in category (*d*), the aside in category (*a*).

Novels, plays etc. are indexed only under their authors. Where, however, Forster refers to a title without having recently mentioned the author, or a fictional character without mentioning the novel, the author, and in the second case the title, can be ascertained from a cross-reference provided in the index.

I have ignored Forster's strictures on chronology to the extent of giving the dates of writers and others. In many cases I have also supplied publication dates – not, however, when (as in the case of Jane Austen) the order of publication is misleadingly different from that of composition. Where serial publication preceded publication in volume form, the earlier date is given.

An 'n' following a page number denotes a footnote; Forster is abbreviated to F. throughout.

OLIVER STALLYBRASS

Lubbock, Percy – *cont.*
  Craft of Fiction (1921), 81, 83,
  137n, 160–61, 167, 186;
  Roman Pictures (1923), 135–6,
  160
Lucas, Charlotte, *see* Austen:
  Pride and Prejudice
Lyons, A. Neil (1880–1940), 37

Magic Flute, see Dickinson
Man Friday, *see* Defoe:
  Robinson Crusoe
Mansfield, Denis, 174
Maran, René (1887–1959 or
  1960): *Batouala: Véritable
  Roman Nègre* (1921; Prix
  Goncourt), 54
Marius the Epicurean, see Pater
marriage: as a way of ending a
  novel, 50, 94
Materials and Methods of Fiction,
  see Hamilton
Matson, Norman: *Flecker's
  Magic* (1926), 107–9
Matthews, James Brander
  (1852–1929; 'perhaps the
  last of the gentlemanly
  school of critics and essayists
  that distinguished American
  literature in the last half of
  the nineteenth centry' –
  *Dictionary of American
  Biography*), 176
Maurois, André (1885–1967),
  56n
Melville, Herman (1819–91),
  126–30, 170–71; *Billy Budd,*
  128–9, 132, 170–71;
  'Hawthorne and his Mosses'
  quoted, 170; *Moby Dick,* 25,
  102, 123, 124 (quotation from
  chapter 85), 126–8, 133, 159,

171, 174, 182–6 *passim; Pierre*
  (quotation from chapter 2),
  31, 171
Memoirs of a Midget, see de la
  Mare
memory: needed to grasp a
  plot, 88–9
Meredith, George (1828–1909),
  62, 89–92, 102, 161; inferior
  to Hardy, 89–90, 92; a
  suburban roarer, 93; uses
  banners, 148; smells, 161;
  Beauchamp's Career (1875), 91,
  148; *The Egoist* (1879), 88,
  91, 148; *Evan Harrington*
  (1861; hero was the son of a
  successful tailor), 74, 137,
  161; *Harry Richmond* (1871),
  90, 103; 'Lucifer in Starlight'
  quoted ('The army of
  unalterable law'), 105; *The
  Ordeal of Richard Feverel*
  (1859), 26; 'The Thrush in
  February' quoted, 89
Micawber, Mr and Mrs, *see*
  Dickens: *David Copperfield*
Middleton, Clara, *see*
  Meredith: *The Egoist*
Milton, John (1608–74), 61–2
mind, *see* human mind
Moby Dick, see Melville
moon, landing on: foreseen, 151
Mozart, Wolfgang Amadeus
  (1757–94), 113
Muddle: the god hidden in
  Tristram Shandy, 106, 125
music: fictional analogies with,
  50–51, 134, 146–9
mystery needed in plot, 88, 91,
  95
mysticism: conceals something,
  123

PENGUIN CLASSICS

www.penguinclassics.com

- *Details about every Penguin Classic*

- *Advanced information about forthcoming titles*

- *Hundreds of author biographies*

- *FREE resources including critical essays on the books and their historical background, reader's and teacher's guides.*

- *Links to other web resources for the Classics*

- *Discussion area*

- *Online review copy ordering for academics*

- *Competitions with prizes, and challenging Classics trivia quizzes*

PENGUIN CLASSICS ONLINE

READ MORE IN PENGUIN

In every corner of the world, on every subject under the sun, Penguin represents quality and variety – the very best in publishing today.

For complete information about books available from Penguin – including Puffins, Penguin Classics and Arkana – and how to order them, write to us at the appropriate address below. Please note that for copyright reasons the selection of books varies from country to country.

In the United Kingdom: Please write to *Dept. EP, Penguin Books Ltd, Bath Road, Harmondsworth, West Drayton, Middlesex UB7 0DA*

In the United States: Please write to *Consumer Services, Penguin Putnam Inc., 405 Murray Hill Parkway, East Rutherford, New Jersey 07073-2136.* VISA and MasterCard holders call 1-800-631-8571 to order Penguin titles

In Canada: Please write to *Penguin Books Canada Ltd, 10 Alcorn Avenue, Suite 300, Toronto, Ontario M4V 3B2*

In Australia: Please write to *Penguin Books Australia Ltd, 487 Maroondah Highway, Ringwood, Victoria 3134*

In New Zealand: Please write to *Penguin Books (NZ) Ltd, Private Bag 102902, North Shore Mail Centre, Auckland 10*

In India: Please write to *Penguin Books India Pvt Ltd, 11 Community Centre, Panchsheel Park, New Delhi 110017*

In the Netherlands: Please write to *Penguin Books Netherlands bv, Postbus 3507, NL-1001 AH Amsterdam*

In Germany: Please write to *Penguin Books Deutschland GmbH, Metzlerstrasse 26, 60594 Frankfurt am Main*

In Spain: Please write to *Penguin Books S. A., Bravo Murillo 19, 1°B, 28015 Madrid*

In Italy: Please write to *Penguin Italia s.r.l., Via Vittorio Emanuele 45/a, 20094 Corsico, Milano*

In France: Please write to *Penguin France, 12, Rue Prosper Ferradou, 31700 Blagnac*

In Japan: Please write to *Penguin Books Japan Ltd, Iidabashi KM-Bldg, 2-23-9 Koraku, Bunkyo-Ku, Tokyo 112-0004*

In South Africa: Please write to *Penguin Books South Africa (Pty) Ltd, P.O. Box 751093, Gardenview, 2047 Johannesburg*

Penguin Classics

THREE TALES
GUSTAVE FLAUBERT

'When she went to church, she would sit gazing at the picture of the Holy Spirit and it struck her that it looked rather like her parrot'

First published in 1877, the *Three Tales*, dominated by questions of doubt, love, loneliness and religious experience, form Flaubert's final great work. 'A Simple Heart' relates the story of Félicité – an uneducated serving-woman who retains her Catholic faith despite a life of desolation and loss. 'The Legend of Saint Julian Hospitator', inspired by a stained-glass window in Rouen cathedral, describes the fate of Julian, a sadistic hunter destined to murder his own parents. The blend of faith and cruelty that dominates this story may also be found in 'Herodias' – a reworking of the tale of Salome and John the Baptist. Rich with a combination of desire, sorrow and faith, these three diverse works are a triumphant conclusion to Flaubert's creative life.

Roger Whitehouse's vibrant new translation captures the exquisite style of the original prose. Geoffrey Wall's introduction considers the inspiration for the tales in the context of Flaubert's life and other work. This edition includes a further reading list and detailed notes.

Translated by Roger Whitehouse

Edited with an introduction by Geoffrey Wall

Penguin Classics

FAUST PART ONE
JOHANN WOLFGANG VON GOETHE

'The hour is come, as master of my fate,
To prove in man the stature of a god'

The medieval myth of Faust's pact with the devil preoccupied Goethe for most of his working life and in the thirty years during which he worked on Part One he reshaped the legend to dramatize his own very personal concerns as a poet. His version depicts Faust as the greatest scholar of his age, master of every branch of learning – from philosophy and law to medicine and theology – only to recognise that the true secrets of existence remain hidden from mankind. To gain this knowledge, he must sacrifice the very thing that makes him human: his own soul. Reflecting Goethe's preoccupation with the exhilaration and terrors of human creativity, *Faust* offers an ironic perspective on the constant striving in the Age of Enlightenment to challenge the limits of man's advancement through art and science.

Translated with an introduction and notes by David Constantine

With a preface by A.S. Byatt

PENGUIN CLASSICS

MAURICE
E. M. FORSTER

'People were all around them, but with eyes that were intensely blue he whispered, "I love you"'

Maurice Hall is a young man who grows up confident in his privileged status and well aware of his role in society. Modest and generally conformist, he nevertheless finds himself increasingly attracted to his own sex. Through Clive, whom he encounters at Cambridge, and through Alec, the gamekeeper on Clive's country estate, Maurice gradually experiences a profound emotional and sexual awakening. A tale of passion, bravery and defiance, this intensely personal novel was completed in 1914 but remained unpublished until after Forster's death in 1970. Compellingly honest and beautifully written, it offers a powerful condemnation of the repressive attitudes of British society, and is at once a moving love story and an intimate tale of one man's erotic and political self-discovery.

The introduction, by David Leavitt, explores the significance of the novel in relation to Forster's own life and as a founding work of modern gay literature. This edition reproduces the Abinger text of the novel, and includes new notes, a chronology and further reading.

Edited with an introduction and notes by David Leavitt

Penguin Classics

A PASSAGE TO INDIA
E. M. FORSTER

'Shrines are fascinating, especially when rarely opened'

When Adela and her elderly companion Mrs Moore arrive in the Indian town of Chandrapore, they quickly feel trapped by its insular and prejudiced British community. Determined to explore the 'real India', they seek the guidance of the charming and mercurial Dr Aziz, a cultivated Indian Muslim. But a mysterious incident occurs while they are exploring the Marabar caves with Aziz, and the well-respected doctor soon finds himself at the centre of a scandal that rouses violent passions among both the British and their Indian subjects. A masterly portrait of a society in the grip of imperialism,

A Passage to India compellingly depicts the fate of individuals caught between the great political and cultural conflicts of the modern world.

The introduction, by Pankaj Mishra, outlines Forster's complex engagement with Indian society and culture. This edition reproduces the Abinger text and notes, and also includes four of Forster's essays on India, a chronology and further reading.

'His great book ... masterly in its prescience and its lucidity' Anita Desai

Edited by Oliver Stallybrass

With an introduction by Pankaj Mishra

PENGUIN CLASSICS

CHEKHOV: A LIFE IN LETTERS
ANTON CHEKHOV

'Medicine is my lawful wedded wife, and literature my mistress. When I've had enough of one, I can go and spend the night with the other'

From his teenage years in provincial Russia to his premature death in 1904, Anton Chekhov wrote thousands of letters to a wide range of correspondents. This fascinating new selection tells Chekhov's story as a man and a writer through affectionate bulletins to his family, insightful discussions of literature with publishers and theatre directors, and tender love letters to his actress wife. Vividly evoking landscapes, people and his daily life, the letters offer revealing glimpses into Chekhov's preoccupations – the onset of tuberculosis, his dual careers as doctor and writer, and his ambivalence about his growing reputation as Russia's foremost playwright and author. This volume takes us inside the mind of one of the world's great writers, and the character that emerges from these pages is resilient, generous, charming and life enhancing.

This is the first uncensored edition of the letters in any language, including previously unpublished material from the Russian archives, and the translation conveys the humour and warmth of Chekhov's prose.

Translated by Rosamund Bartlett and Anthony Phillips

With an introduction and notes by Rosamund Bartlett

PENGUIN CLASSICS

THE PENGUIN BOOK OF RUSSIAN SHORT STORIES

'Light's all very well, brothers, but it's not easy to live with'

From the early nineteenth century to the collapse of the Soviet Union and beyond, the short story has occupied a central place in Russian literature. This collection includes not only well-known classics but also modern masterpieces, many of them previously censored. There are stories by acknowledged giants – Gogol, Tolstoy, Chekhov and Solzhenitsyn – and by equally great writers such as Andrey Platonov who have only recently become known to the English-speaking world. Some stories are tragic, but the volume also includes a great deal of comedy – from Pushkin's subtle wit to Kharms's dark absurdism, from Dostoyevsky's graveyard humour to Teffi's subtle evocations of human stupidity and Zoshchenko's satirical vignettes of everyday life in the decade after the 1917 Revolution.

This new collection of translations includes works only recently rediscovered in Russia. The introduction gives a vivid insight into the history of the Russian short story, while the work of every author is preceded by an individual introduction. This edition also includes notes and a chronology.

Edited by Robert Chandler